The Guerrilla Rep:
American Film Market Distribution Success on No Budget

2nd Edition

Ben Yennie

DEDICATION

This book is dedicated to my loving and supportive parents and my inspiring and nurturing mentors without all of whom this book would not have been possible.

Additionally, the second edition of this book is also dedicated to my Friend family and Karaoke family here in San Francisco. You all mean more to me than I can say.

Additional Resources Available
TheGuerrillaRep.com

Packet Includes

More distributor and sales agent interviews
Advance contact tracking template
Money saving links for AFM and business travel
Exclusive discounts on film industry workshops
Additional exclusive content: updated regularly!

Download FREE at
www.TheGuerrillaRep.com/Resources

Are you a Film School Teacher?

Given both of my parents were teachers, I'm a huge supporter of higher education. Much to my delight, the first edition of this book was used as both required and recommended reading in film schools nationwide.

So with the second edition, I've decided to run a contest for every semester: one for fall, one for spring, and one for summer. This contest may iterate faster than this book does, so most of the details will be found through the link below.

This contest is meant to be something that could be integrated easily as an extra credit project, as well as teach a useful skill to each student.

There will be prizes given on both a national and school-by-school basis. Prizes will most likely include free workshops, free books, and free software licenses. The student who wins the national prize will also win something for their school.

For more information and to register your school please visit

www.ProducerFoundry.com/FilmSchools

CONTENTS

SECTION 3 – POST-AFM

SECTION 4 – THE CHANGING FACE OF INDIEFILM, AND ADVICE FROM DISTRIBUTORS, SALES AGENTS AND , and FINANCIERS

PREFACE TO THE SECOND EDITION

Reading Ben's book is a must for anyone who is planning to make or find distribution for an independent feature film. While the distribution part of filmmaking seems to fall at the end of the process, it is just the beginning. It should be the cart before the horse on your project. There are many rows to hoe in the fields of finding money for a film project, getting it into production, getting it cut, then finding distribution. Film Festivals with markets or the markets themselves can be helpful to this process when played right. They can also be brutal and insane. The Guerrilla Rep helps round the sharp edges of navigating this world. Don't leave home before reading – it will save you grief, time, and above all, money. And while your successes or failures ride entirely on you, Ben's book can help you plan your direction and hopefully guide you around the pitfalls of the process. Read on and be well.

--Debbie Brubaker
Producer, Line Producer, UPM

The Guerrilla Rep
AFM Success on No Budget

FOREWORD

In the opening pages of his new book, **The Guerrilla Rep: AFM Success on No Budget,** Ben Yennie writes: "... the people who need to attend AFM are producers. directors and actors will go, but the people who will get business done are producers." In the film and entertainment industries, it is the work of producers that drives the bulk of business and financing activities, and there's likely no better place for an emerging producer to experience trial-by-fire than the legendary American Film Market.

With this in mind, Yennie has crafted a nuanced how-to guide for producers that is both practical and personal. By all appearances, Yennie is a young, up and coming producer himself, and he knows that being a first timer at such a large industry event with many influencers can be daunting. Using his own experience as a backdrop for the AFM attendee, he shares insightful steps for the newcomer that can turn your first time at the AFM into an unprecedented opportunity to learn, grow and push yourself.

The big take away from this read is that every attendee should have a very clear game plan in place before heading to the AFM. And, while this may sound a bit "captain obvious," Yennie's guide reminds the producer that one's game plan needs to include some important things like -- building your personal brand and managing your mindset. On the former, he writes, "When you're building your personal brand, the most important thing is that this brand is still you. Distinctively, unapologetically you. People can always tell when your mask gets too thick and they don't like it. Branding doesn't ever mean you should do something that doesn't jive with who you are." Sage advice, especially in an industry that ultimately responds to one extremely essential item -- TALENT.

All in all, this book serves as a no-budget roadmap, something which is tough to achieve when attending film industry events. The amount of expenses and out-of-pocket that comes with attending any film market will require each attendee to cherry pick where and how to spend. In this regard, Yennie's lists are clever, funny and chock full of tips and tricks that leave helpful room for interpretation and handprint, a key piece of the puzzle that any good resource allows for.

But, what's really helpful here is Yennie's approach to outlining the most effective ways to think about the market -- before, during and after. For Yennie, the combined approach to preparation, interaction and follow-up is an artform, and he peppers his analysis with several eye opening question and answer dialogues with key industry leaders -- each of whom offers up tangible advice for the newbie. These sections point out in a candid way that being a newbie is definitely NOT a bad thing. However, being a newbie who is ill informed, posturing hubris, or lacking social skills won't win over anyone. In Yennie's view, your first AFM is simply just that -- the first of many markets you're likely to attend over the arc of a long and lively career. It's a significant point of entry. A chance to build credibility, relationships, and, yes, even trust.

The key thing to remember when using any how-to guide is that no one person holds the secrets to success. Yennie acknowledges that each producer will come to a market like the AFM with his or her own goals. But, having a handbook that outlines some helpful rules of the road can be an invaluable resource. Now, that you have one, go forth and start being the producer that you know you can be. The one who is authentic, heartfelt and poised for greatness.

-- Marc Smolowitz
Director, Producer, Executive Producer
13th Gen, San Francisco

PROLOGUE

There are many things this book is not. This is not a book about revenue projections. It is not a book that will tell you how to schedule and budget your film. And it is not a book that will teach you to write a business plan. There are many books on every one of those subjects written better than I could write them at this juncture. This is a book for a much narrower subject; a subject that can take those things you learned in film school and transform them from good information into something you can build a career on. This is a guide to using the American Film Market to find distribution for your projects.

WHAT IS THE AMERICAN FILM MARKET?

For short, it's called AFM. It is the biggest gathering of Sales Agents, international buyers, and filmmakers in the United States. It is held the first or second week of November every year in Santa Monica, CA. It's a place filmmakers can go to meet with distributors, sales agents, and international buyers. Simply put, it's the best place you can go as an American filmmaker to get your film into the hands of distributors and sales agents.

Even more so than the film industry at large, international sales is a business that relies heavily on relationships. International sales agents are able to sell their products because they've spent decades cultivating relationships with buyers. Markets like AFM are necessary to maintain those relationships, because they provide much needed chances for face-to-face interactions.

ARE MARKETS EVEN RELEVANT ANY MORE?

Much of the market is shifting towards VOD, but even with that, there are still gatekeepers for the platforms you really want to be on – which still requires knowing someone on the inside. If you can become a face at the market, you're more likely to make friends with the people you need to know who can get you on those platforms.

Additionally, most of the real money for independent film is in television, and the competing and associated subscription video on demand platforms that go with it. If you want to make enough money in independent film to make it a fruitful career, you need to spend a lot of time building a relationship with your audience. Getting your film on Netflix, Amazon Prime, or HBO can help you greatly expand both your reputation and your reach.

WHY SHOULD YOU GO?

There's a sad truth many filmmakers don't want to accept: There is no money in filmmaking. If you make a film, you'll just spend a lot of money. The only money to be made is in SELLING your film. That's the biggest reason to go to AFM; the people who can help you sell your project are there.

You should go to AFM because if you want to be a professional producer, the contacts you make and the relationships you build there will quickly become the most valuable asset in your company. Everyone knows the adage, "it's not what you know, it's who you know". The people you need to know attend the American Film Market. They're not always easy to approach, and they're not always easy to get a meeting with, but you've got a far better chance of doing business with them if you've met them. And the place to meet them is at AFM.

You're probably not going to close any deals on your first outing to AFM, but if you want to close deals at all, it will be far easier if you've actually met the people you're dealing with. Although if you do your research and advance contact correctly, you may get an offer shortly after the market closes. I've helped a few clients to do so. There's a lot of psychology behind this idea which gets rather complex and goes far beyond the scope of this book, but meeting someone in person is a much better way to open a business relationship than almost any other way. This is especially true in the film industry.

In order to build a good business relationship, one must understand what's in it for both parties. Distributors and Sales agents go to AFM for three reasons. First, they want to sell the films already in their catalog. You should always remember that, and be happy about it because once your film is in their catalog it's exactly what you'll want them to do. Second, they want to acquire completed films to sell at future markets. Finally, they want to build relationships with producers in order to build a pipeline for future projects they'll want to sell. That is a prioritized list of why distributors attend AFM, and you should keep it in mind during your preparation.

WHO SHOULD GO?

On the filmmaker side, the people who need to attend AFM are producers. Directors and actors will go, but the people who will get business done are producers and executive producers. If you're a director, the veterans will know you're looking for work. You may well find work, but you won't sell any movies. Actors may find work as well, but these are things everyone who attends the market should keep in mind.

If you're a producer, you'll learn more about the way the industry actually works in the week you're there than you did in years of film school. Truly understanding AFM — the American Film Market — is something you can only do by attending the Market. Now before you put this book back on the shelf, there are things that you can learn from it. This book will teach you what you need to know before you go. Since initial publication, I've been recognized more times than I can count based on the first edition of the book.

HOW DOES THIS BOOK HELP?

There are many tricks to getting the most out of the market, and I've written this book to share those tricks with you. I want you to get the most out of your attendance at AFM, even if it's your first time. I generally say that my first time to AFM marked my transition from amateur to professional. That is true for many producers, even those who have already completed a feature. Because, again, you cannot make money when you make a film. You only make money when you sell it.

One of the most important things to remember about AFM is that your productivity will build exponentially each year you attend. For instance, in my first year, I had very little idea what I was doing. At the end of the week I walked out with only 20-30 new contacts, but I had gained a much better idea of how the market worked.

My second year I was much more comfortable; I devoted more time to preparing, researching, and planning. I ended up with around fifty new contacts and a distribution deal that year. My third year, I went in with one new distribution deal, and I walked out with over a hundred and fifty new contacts. Of these, over twenty of them were buyers, and over thirty were distribution and acquisitions managers. By the end of the market my third year, I had Sales Agents calling me about my projects with no attachments in the script stage.

In my fourth year, I went to market with five completed features and came home with fifty-five screener requests from over fifteen different sales agents. I also added over two hundred new contacts to my phone book.

In my fifth year – the year after this book was published – I increased the value of my personal brand exponentially, and made several much higher level contacts than I had before, including the managing director of AFM, Jonathan Wolf.

In my sixth year, I attended the market as an exhibitor. I had a movie already being sold in another office, and between advance contact and follow-up, I had a 120% offer rate, which ended up with around a 100% close rate, including a sale to a Starz. How do you end up with a 120% offer rate? You acquire a movie while you're at the market, then turn around and place it during after-market follow-up.

There is a strategy that my company implemented that has proven successful. That's why I'm writing this book. I'm going to share the tips, tricks, and hacks I learned at the American Film Market – tricks that can lead to your success. And I'm going to teach you how to turn your trip from an expensive working vacation to a successful business venture from which you can build a career.

In the end, AFM is really about making and developing relationships. While cultivating relationships is important in any business, it's particularly vital in the film industry. This book is a guide to using this unfamiliar environment to build relationships and create a better business.

HOW DO I USE THIS BOOK?

This book is comprised of three parts. The first is the pre-AFM work: the preparation and advance contact you'll do to allow you the best possible chance of success at the market. The second is a guide for how you'll spend your time at the market. The third will help you follow up after the market. This book is primarily written for those who have yet to go to AFM, however if you've gone once or twice and not gotten the success you'd hoped for, this book might also be able to help you.

Read this book before or during each section of the market the book is titled for. I recommend reading the whole book a few months before you go to the market and referring back to the appropriate section as you go through each stage of your preparation and attendance. The short chapters are designed for easy reference before, during, and after.

Bring this book to AFM, but don't get caught reading it at the market. You want to appear to be a pro, even if it's your first day. In business and at AFM, image is everything and people only want to work with professionals. Read it in the solitude of your hotel room or your AirBnB if you have questions or are uncertain what to do next.

A NOTE ON THE SECOND EDITION

When this book was first published, it was the first book seeking to give filmmakers a guide to understanding the culture of film markets. It was written as a guide to understanding AFM before your first trip. Much to my surprise and delight, I have had many people including a good portion of AFM veterans say how much the book has helped them.

The first edition even ended up being used as recommended or required reading in more than ten film schools.

It's been two years and two markets since the initial publication, so it seemed prudent to update the text. I've learned much between these publications and grown my career significantly due largely to continued attendance of the American Film Market. This edition comes with an additional two years of wisdom, experience, and growth that I seek to share with you.

Self-righteous pomposity aside, there are also several new and fun stories I wanted to share. That content includes some additional related articles from my blog that have been updated and made more relevant to this book.

More info, tools, and resources at www.TheGuerrillaRep.com.

Due to page and word count restrictions, as well as inherent limitations of a paperback book, I've made some additional content available through my website. This content is free, and includes additional information, tools, and resources which will make preparing for AFM go much more smoothly for you.

You can find them at **www.TheGuerrillaRep.com/resources**

SECTION 1: PRE-AFM

CHAPTER 1 – WHAT IS A FILM MARKET, ANYWAY?

After the prologue, you have a 50,000 foot view of AFM. Let's zoom in a tad and check out a bit more about the total landscape of Film Markets in general, as well as the sales cycle for them.

WHAT'S THE DIFFERENCE BETWEEN A FILM MARKET AND A FILM FESTIVAL?

When speaking, I get asked this question more than any other, with one possible exception that will be covered in the next chapter.

Put simply, a film festival is a celebration of the artistry of film. Film markets are centered around the commerce of film. Film festivals are about the pageantry of film and film markets are about the business of it. Some festivals have a lot of crossover, like Sundance and Toronto. Some film festivals have markets attached. AFM is attached to the AFI Fest, Berlinale is attached to the European Film Market, and the Cannes Film Festival has the biggest film market in the world attached: Marché du Film.

The biggest difference between a film festival and a film market is the focus of the two. When most people think of Cannes, they think of the festival, not the market. However anyone involved in distribution thinks the opposite. While the festival is full of red carpets and pageantry, the market side is much more about the business behind the scenes. More money flies around at Marché du Film than almost anywhere else in the word, at least in regards to the film industry.

Of course, I'm not trying to underplay the importance of film festivals. They serve a vital role in the promotion of the film. If used properly, they can greatly increase the visibility and marketability of the film, particularly if you're self-distributing. The bigger festivals will even help you get your film sold, or at least increase the sale price.

However, speaking solely in regards to international sales, the only festivals that really matter are top-tier festivals. These are festivals like Sundance, Tribeca, Toronto, and Cannes. Other festivals can help to raise your social media presence and marketing proliferation, but they won't increase your international sales price in a meaningful way.

There's already a book on film festivals. Chris Gores wrote it better than I could. You can find a helpful link to that in the resource packet at TheGuerrillaRep.com.

WHAT ARE THE OTHER FILM MARKETS?

While AFM is the biggest narrative feature film focused market in the US, there are many more media markets across the country and across the globe. Here are fourteen film and TV markets you should know about, though there are many more.   Markets generally take place anywhere between a few days and a week around the same time every year. Here's a handy-dandy table for reference.

Market Name	Location	When	Primarily for
American Film Market (AFM)	Santa Monica, California	November	Narrative Features, esp genre pics.
CineMart	Rotterdam, Netherlands	January	Co-Production
European Film Market (EFM)	Berlin, Germany	February	Narrative Features, esp genre pics

Market Name	Location	When	Primarily for
Hong Kong International Film & TV Market (FILMART)	Hong Kong	March	
Hot Docs	Toronto, Canada	April/May	Documentaries
Independent Film Week (Formerly IFP)	Ney York City, New York	September	
Marché du Film (Associated with Cannes IFF)	**Cannes, France**	**May**	**Narrative Features**
MIPCOM	Cannes, France	October	Television, Documentaries
MIPTV	Cannes, France	April	Television
National Media Market (NMM)	Charleston, South Carolina	November	
NAPTE	Miami, Florida	January	Television
Sunny Side of the Doc	La Rochelle, France	June	Documentaries
TIFFCOM (Content Market at The Tokyo IFF)	Tokyo, Japan	October	

HOW MANY FILM MARKETS DOES A SALES AGENT GO TO IN A YEAR?

Any good sales agent will go to at least the three major markets. Those would be AFM, EFM, and Marché du Film. If they're not attending at least those three, it's probably not a good idea to sign with them. It is better if they go to other markets as well, since it often takes as many as five face-to-face touch points to get a sale.

As such, even if you can get your film placed at AFM, it may take a while to get your money back. Sometimes as much as a full market cycle.

Producer's reps are a bit different. Producer's reps take a bit less of a cut to sell domestically and a much smaller cut to hand off to a sales agent. Since they maintain relationships primarily with sales agents, they can get away with only attending one or two of those markets.

HOW MANY FILM MARKETS SHOULD FILMMAKERS ATTEND IN A YEAR?

Well, that's a tricky question. There's some very high level networking to be had at such a convention, but beyond that there's not always a great way to justify it as an ongoing expense.

I'd say a producer should attend several markets throughout the course of their career, just so they know what's entailed in one. That said, they only consistently attend the closest one to them. If you're looking to be a powerful executive producer or studio head, then you will need to spend time traveling to all of them, but if you just want to make movies, you're probably alright only regularly attending one.

CHAPTER 2 – WHAT'S THE DIFFERENCE BETWEEN A SALES AGENT AND A DISTRIBUTOR?

When I wrote the first edition of this book, I didn't realize exactly how opaque the waters of film finance and distribution truly are. But when the most common question I would be asked at speaking engagements became 'What's the difference between a sales agent and a distributor?', I thought it would make sense to include a breakdown of the major distribution players in the second edition. Pieces of this chapter and some great images are available on my website, www.TheGuerrillaRep.com.

DISTRIBUTOR / BUYER

A distributor is someone who takes the product to an end user. This can be anything from a buyer for a theater chain, PayTV channel, or VOD platform, to an entertainment media buyer for a large retail chain like Wal-Mart, Target, or Walgreens. The rights that distributors take are generally broken up both by media type and by territory.

For Instance, if you were to sell a film to someone like HBO, they would likely take at least the US PayTV and SVOD rights, so that it could stream on premium television and HBO Go/Now. They make take additional territories as well – potentially even the world.

Conversely, it's not uncommon to sell all of France or Germany in one go. Rights should be and often are sold by language, so sometimes French Canada will sell with France. Although as of late, Canada often sells as its own territory. Typically, it's the sales agent's job to separate those rights in the most advantageous ways.

Generally these entities will pay real money via a wire transfer and almost always will only deal directly with a sales agent. Sometimes territorial buyers will deal directly with a producer's rep, although generally that's more common with domestic rather than international buyers. VOD platforms will generally deal with an aggregator due to some rather complex technical issues that arise from streaming content online. The traditional model of independent film financing is built around presales to these sorts of entities, but that presale model has recently shifted.

There are also some DIY distribution platforms that will enable you to get DVDS in bookstores, but we'll be covering that more in the last chapter of Section 3.

SALES AGENT

A sales agent is a person or company with deep connections into the world of international sales. They specialize in segmenting and selling rights to individual territories. Often, they will be distributors themselves within their country of origin. This business is entirely relationship-based and the sales agents who have been around a while have very long-term business relationships with buyers all around the world. That's why they travel to all of the major film markets.

Examples on the medium-large end would be Magnolia Pictures International, Tri-Coast Entertainment, and Multivisionnaire. WonderPhil is up and coming as well. The Weinstein Company, Lionsgate, and Focus Features would also be considered distributors/sales agents, but they're very hard to approach.

Generally, these sales specialists will work on commission. They may offer a minimum guarantee when you sign the film, but that is not common. Typically, they will charge recoupable expenses that mean you won't see any money until after they're recouped a certain amount. There are ways around this, but I'll touch on this in a later chapter. Their commission will be between 20% and 35%. This is variable depending on several factors, but generally 25% or under is good. Anything over 30% is a sign you should do some extra diligence on this sales agent and negotiate the deal a bit as much as you can.

AGGREGATORS

Aggregators are companies that help you get on VOD platforms. The most important service they provide is helping you conform to technical specifications required by various VOD platforms. This job is not as easy as you would think it is, which is why they charge so much. Additionally, they have better access to some VOD platforms than others. These days, it's very difficult to get on iTunes without one.

They generally charge a not-insubstantial fee to get you on these platforms, and they offer little to help you market the project. Companies like this include Distribbr, Bitmax, as well as several others in the resource packet.

There are merits to going this route, but they can be expensive, often costing about one thousand USD up front and growing from there. A more thorough analysis can be found in the resource packet.

PRODUCER OF MARKETING AND DISTRIBUTION (PMD)

In the words of Former ICM agent Jim Jeramanok, PMDs are worth their weight in gold. A PMD is a producer who helps you develop your marketing and social media strategy, your festival strategy, and your distribution strategy. They're also quite likely to have some connections into distribution. They're there to give your film the best possible chance at making money when it's done.

Generally, they're paid just as any other producer would be, but if they're good, they're worth every penny. With a good PMD on board, your project's chances for monetary success are exponentially better. If you're an investor reading this, you want any film you invest in to at least have access to a PMD or producer's rep.

EXECUTIVE PRODUCER

In the independent film world, the traditional definition of an executive producer is someone who helps you package projects by attaching distribution, bankable talent, and (with luck) financing. They'll also help you design a beneficial financial mix (I.E. where can you best utilize tax incentives, presales, brand integration, equity, and gap debt) in order to help your project have the best chance of success.

Often, they'll take a percentage of your raise and you'll have to have some money to pay them up front.   Not an insane amount of money, but some.

PRODUCER'S REP

Simply put, a producer's rep is somewhat of a mix between a PMD and an executive producer.   A producer's rep takes on a lot of the business development jobs for a film. We wear a lot of hats. Most often we'll connect filmmakers with completed projects to sales agents and negotiate the best possible deal. We're skilled negotiators with a deep knowledge of the film distribution scene and entrenched connections there.

If a producer's rep comes on in the beginning, we'll do the job of an executive producer. We'll help you finance the film in the best way possible. Not just through equity investment, but planning proper utilization of tax incentives, pre-sales, crowdfunding, occasional product placement, and sometimes helping connect you to some of our angel contacts.   That said, if we've never met, you have no track record, and you want us to start raising money for you, that probably won't happen.

Not all producer's reps will work with first-time directors and producers. I will, but generally only on completed projects or projects near the end of post-production. I will not help someone who I have not worked with before garner investment for their projects, except in very limited circumstances. I will help filmmakers get their financial mix in order. If a rep makes connections for investment, we need to know the filmmakers we're working with can deliver a quality product and get our investment contacts their money back.

A good producer's rep will also be able to act as a PMD, or at least refer you to a good one. We don't just work in traditional distribution, but can help plan and implement other tactics including proper use of VOD. We'll help you plan your marketing and distribution and then we'll tell you how to implement it, helping you along the way. We'll help you develop the best package in order to mitigate the risk taken by our investors. If we do bring on investors, you'd best believe we're with you through the end of the project, to make sure that everyone ends up better off. We'll check in and act as a coach to help you grow to the next level.

In a lot of ways, we're agents for producers and films. Good reps, like good agents, won't just think about this project; we'll help you use your projects to move to the next step in your career.

So how do you pay a producer's rep? Since the services we offer are so varied, our pay scale is as well. Some things are based primarily on commission. This is generally for brokering tasks like connecting to a sales agent, although sometimes we have to charge a non-refundable deposit for those tasks. That commission is generally around 10%, but can range between 5-15%. Some things (like document and plan creation) are a flat fee. Others are hourly plus commission on completion. That would apply primarily to packaging.

It is worth noting that not all producer's reps are trustworthy. There are some that charge 5 figures up front with no guarantee of performance. Admittedly, no one can guarantee they can sell your film, or get it financed through angel investment. If they guarantee it and ask for a large upfront payment, you should be very wary of them. However, there are some with a strong track record of doing so. Just as you would when talking with sales agents, make sure you do your due diligence and talk with some of their previous clients.

CHAPTER 3 – BADGES AND BADGE STRATEGY

Before jumping into the badges of AFM, I believe a brief breakdown of AFM's schedule would be helpful. AFM runs from Wednesday to Tuesday. Generally by Tuesday afternoon, most of the offices are already being packed up and the people you would want to meet are already packing it in. However, you will sometimes find people who will take a meeting on Wednesday. If you're travelling from outside LA, you should allot Wednesday morning for meetings, but plan to fly out in the afternoon.

Distributors will not want to talk to you about acquiring new projects before the last two or three days of the market. The rest of the time they'll be talking to buyers. This knowledge will inform your badge strategy.

When you plan your AFM trip, you'll have to decide which badge will be most useful and cost effective. While it may seem that your badge strategy could vary, the most likely scenario is in your first year at AFM you should get the cheapest badge available. This is primarily because of those three sales agent and distributor priorities laid out in the prologue. Remember? One – sell their catalogue. Two – acquire completed films. Three – build relationships for the future. Generally, the Industry Badge will suit a new producer's needs perfectly.

This stated, if you're not accustomed or familiar with the inner workings and business of the Film Industry, it may be wise to attend the AFM Conference Series, as it will give you valuable insights, and is generally one of the most up-to-date sources available. For most of the people reading this book, they can be very useful. You may want to consider live-tweeting them, as you'll learn a fair amount and it can really help enhance your social media presence.

Here's a brief rundown on what badges are available for AFM, and what each of the colors indicate. Since the prices and cutoff dates vary a bit every year, you can find that information on the AFM website or in the resource packet. Do know, buying your badge early can save you a lot of money, as there are two cutoff dates where prices increase each year. All badges now offer free WiFi for up to two devices.

INDUSTRY PASS BADGE

The most common badge is the red badge, also known as the Industry Badge. These are the least expensive and also the least exclusive. They give you access to the major floors, but little else. This badge is also only active during the last three days – Sunday to Tuesday. You don't need to be an IFTA member to get one.

What's IFTA you ask? IFTA is the Independent Film and Television Alliance, and they are the organization that puts on the AFM. In order to be a member, you must have distributed at least 3 films within the last twelve months. Membership is quite expensive, with introductory membership costing over $9,000 a year for the first 4 years, and $6,000 a year after that. These are the people who are eligible to be buyers and make their living distributing films.

INDUSTRY PASS PLUS BADGE

The next level is the Industry Pass Plus. The Industry Pass Plus allows access to the last four days of the market, plus four days of conferences. Depending on your experience, the conferences can be very valuable. They can allow you access to speakers who can be excellent contacts. Depending on your networking style and access to similar conferences and seminars, it can be worth the additional cost to attend the conferences.

EXECUTIVE PASS BADGE

The mid-range attendee badge level is the Executive Pass, which allows you access to all floors at the American Film Market for the entire market. It's a pretty big price hike to purchase this badge. Honestly there are very few situations where you would need the Executive Pass, given that distributors and Sales Agents don't really want to talk about acquiring new projects until the end of the market. This will be discussed in later chapters.

EXECUTIVE PLUS BADGE

As with the Industry Pass Plus, there's also the Executive Pass Plus. The only difference between the Executive Pass and the Executive Pass Plus is that the Executive Pass Plus allows access to all of the conferences. While I generally attend primarily for the networking opportunities, these conferences can be valuable. This badge, and all the badges listed above are red badges.

PLATINUM BADGE

Finally, the most expensive and exclusive of the attendee badges is the Platinum Badge. Second only to the Exhibitor Badge, it is the most expensive badge offered to attendees by AFM. In addition to access to all of the conferences, it also allows access to the buyer's lounge. The buyer's lounge offers free black and white printing.

Despite the cost, do consider this: access to the buyers lounge offers better access to buyers. Although, it's not as useful as you may think. Most of the buyers go to the lounge to review their potential acquisitions, and take a break from the market. With that in mind it's not a great place to network. The biggest advantage to the platinum badge is some additional networking opportunities offered by the AFM parties.

As you'd expect, this badge is platinum colored, although it looks a little more grey given the matte printing.

EXHIBITOR BADGE

Next is the purple Exhibitor Badge. If you're wearing a red badge, purple badges are decorating the people you'll want to talk to, but generally not until the last couple days of the market. Exhibitors are often people who have paid to have offices at AFM. There are too many office plans to really go through in this book, but once you factor in staff, travel, furniture rental, and advertising, an office rental can easily cost in the 5 figures on the lower end, sometimes even well into six figures on the high end. Each office price covers the admittance of two or three people to the market, although exhibitors can buy additional badges and many of them do.

For most people, the expense simply isn't practical, unless you have at least a few films that you're trying to sell to buyers at the market, or perhaps one big film you've already completed and need to sell. This badge is really for sales agents and US distributors. The best reason to be familiar with this badge is if you're looking to get a distribution deal for a completed film, these are some of the people you'll want to talk to.

A lot of exhibitors are members of IFTA, but not all. It will say whether or not they are on their badge, so you can tell, just by looking, whether they've been screened or not. There are a lot of sharks in the pool that is AFM and IFTA membership is one way of screening them out. This is not fool-proof, but it certainly helps.

SHARED OFFICES BELOW THE LOBBY

Starting in 2014, AFM began offering booths on the third floor to producers looking to establish relationships with sales agents and sell their films. This offering has been taken advantage of both for newer producers, and as a lower cost option for other exhibitors. This option can be really good for production companies looking to attend AFM, as it gives you a base of operations for working the market.

Another excellent strategy for new filmmakers is to book a screening at AFM. A screening like this can help greatly in selling your film. It gives an excellent place to invite sales agents so that you can meet them in person and talk to them about your project. It's generally better to hold a screening like this on the last few days of the market, so they can come once they've done their selling.

There are a few other benefits to having this level of badge. Apart from access to the buyer's lounge, it gives you a base of operations and it makes it much easier to meet with people. Additionally, if you are looking to sell your films to buyers at AFM, then this badge is a necessity. Buyers don't really want to talk to you if you don't have an office.

It is best to book this badge early, as they do run out of offices. I went to AFM 2015 as an exhibitor, but due to the late booking I ended up with a purple badge and no office. That made my job very difficult.

However there were other benefits. Exhibitors get contact information for a shocking amount of buyers. It is important to state that this contact information doesn't do you a whole lot of good if you haven't met the people in person. As stated in Chapter 1, this business really is about relationships. An email and phone number won't do you much good if you haven't looked the person in the eye and talked to them.

BUYER BADGES

Finally, there are the Green Buyer Badges. Green Badges are the people everybody wants to talk to, but they may not want to talk to you. A Buyer Badge allows access to the entire market and of course, the buyer's lounge.

As stated before, a buyer is generally a representative of a media outlet. These people have to buy a lot of content, so they don't have time to deal with people who don't know what they're doing. As such, most buyers don't want to deal with anyone except a sales agent.

DAY BADGES

There are a couple other badges that bear mentioning. There is a Single Day Badge, which costs $250 and allows access for one particular day of the market. They change color depending on the day. Frankly, I see little point in most people buying these badges, unless you need to be at the market for a single day to take a meeting.

They're great if you're only going to be in Santa Monica on a particular day, especially in the early days of the market, but two of them costs more than an Industry Plus Badge, which gives you access to the last four days of the market and four conferences. And remember, the people you probably want to see will not be ready to see you earlier than that.

PRESS BADGES

There is also the orange Press Badge. This book isn't really targeted for members of the press, but there are advantages to having a Press Badge. The biggest reason to keep your eyes out for orange badges is that the wearers can be really good contacts to help you break your film and get it some publicity. Generally the press doesn't want to talk to filmmakers, but if you happen to catch a press person relaxing and can strike up a good conversation, it can be rewarding.

Also, the Press Badge is free, so if you happen to have a contact with a paper that could give you an assignment letter to cover AFM it can be a good way to get access to the market. That said, a Press Badge will often limit the interactions you have with exhibitors and buyers, so it's not always a good idea to get one, even if you can.

They won't give you a Press Badge just because you have a blog or a podcast. They will give you one if you have enough followers on that blog or podcast, though. They have very clear requirements on the website.

STAFF BADGES

The blue Security/Staff Badges are something you'll want to keep an eye out for. There are a lot of little rules about AFM that you need to be aware of and you need to make sure you stay on the good side of the security guys. If you don't, they can make your life and your sales very difficult.

Generally speaking, security is there to help and make sure that nothing untoward is going on in the lobby, or in the market as a whole. Although I've had some run ins with them from hustling a little too hard with the wrong size of printed materials. More on that in the printed materials section.

BADGE STRATEGY

So now that you know what badges there are to choose from, what do you do with that information? Well, which badge you should get is highly dependent on your situation. If it's your first time at the American Film Market, more than likely the best badge for you is going to be either the Industry or the Industry Plus Badge. Even though you'll only have your badge for the second half of the market, you should attend for the entire market.

MARKET HACK #1 – WORK THE WHOLE MARKET

This brings me to the first secret of working AFM. You DO NOT need a badge to get into the lobby. Now some of you reading this may be thinking, so what? Why would I want to spend four days sitting in the lobby of a hotel? Trust me, that is exactly where you want to be and what you want to be doing.

I did not do so my first year. I was only there about half a day before my badge kicked in. While I had some meetings, it wasn't an overwhelmingly successful AFM. My second year, the only reason I walked out with a distribution deal was that I talked to somebody in the lobby who told me to talk to the Sales Agent he was working with. When my badge kicked in, we went down to make a meeting. When we walked out of the meeting, we had a distribution deal. Time and time again people tell me that the most success they saw was due to spending time in the lobby, and it's true.

That said, this tactic isn't as good as it used to be. As of 2014, you need a badge to access the pool area. Due to this, the pool has become much more enjoyable if you have a badge, and the lobby much more crowded if you don't.

That said, you probably won't close any deals in the lobby. Remember those Blue Staff Badges? That's security, and they don't like it when you hand out anything bigger than a business card. So it's very important to get a badge for the latter half of the market so you can go in and make deals with the people whose hand you shook in the lobby those first few days.

You could get a badge for the full market, but unless you're a buyer, most of the exhibitors won't want to see you until the end of the market, anyway. Save your money and put it into higher quality printed materials or into getting an AFM-affiliated hotel (which will eliminate your need for a rental car). Once you pick up your badge, you'll want to set as many meetings as possible once the market opens for you. The biggest advantage to the Industry Plus Badge is the fact that you get to make meetings a day earlier than the people with the standard industry badges and you get fantastic information from the AFM conference series. If you've a little bit more of a budget, then it's a good way to go.

If you've got a larger-budgeted film that's been completed, then there may be wisdom in getting an office on the second floor of the Loews Hotel. However, that is quite expensive and if it's your first outing to the market I don't recommend it. On the other hand, if you've got somebody who's been a few times and has a decent list of contacts, it might be worth considering. Generally it's too large an expense for a single film, which is why distributors and sales agents are most often selling slates.

So, now you've decided which badge to get. What's next?

CHAPTER 4 – HOTELS AND AirBnB

There are several things to consider when booking your hotel at AFM. The biggest consideration is whether or not you're going to have a car. While the AFM-sponsored hotels are fantastic, they're about twice as expensive as the other hotels. They do provide a nice sense of inclusion and the shuttle system for AFM is helpful. Speaking as a proud San Franciscan, it can be a huge load off your mind if you don't need a car, and depending where you're coming from it can make your life a lot easier.

The other consideration about the AFM hotels and the shuttles is that there is excellent networking to be found on said shuttles. I met a couple of distributors on the shuttle and after building a bit of a rapport set a meeting with them at the end of the market. One is now a valued contact that ended up speaking at a seminar I organized.

If you're driving, there's little point in getting an AFM-affiliated hotel. Since there's a shuttle from the AFM Parking lot, you'll still get some networking to and from the market. You can get a parking pass that allows you to come and go from the lot as much as you like, but you're probably better off paying the fee at the lot for parking on a daily basis. That means you'll need to carry cash, but it's cheaper to do things this way. The AFM-affiliated hotels can be booked when you purchase your badge, which takes a step out of your planning, although it's not difficult to book a hotel online.

If you're not driving down, the exorbitant car rental fees are about equal to the difference between staying at an affiliate hotel and staying off-site. It just depends where you want to spend your money. Would you rather spend your money to be in a nicer AFM affiliated hotel, or spend it on the freedom and versatility offered by a rental car?

When booking your hotel, you should be aware that not all hotels are clean and that many of the bargain options in LA and Santa Monica have pests. This is not true of all bargain hotels, and the tourism commission probably won't like me being this honest about it, but it's true. Also, be aware that many of the non-AFM-affiliated hotels near the Loews Hotel are booked 6-9 months in advance. Planning ahead and booking hotels far in advance will give you a much better chance at getting a good price on a hotel. The simple fact that all the AFM-affiliated hotels are clean and inspected is a huge advantage. Also, you never know whom you'll meet in the hallways.

A friend and mentor of mine, Bill, actually got a meeting specifically because he was staying in an AFM-affiliated hotel. His name is very common and apparently there is a buyer that shares both his first and last name. He got a letter under his door from a higher-end distributor looking to make a meeting with him. Even though the distributor realized they made a mistake when he called, they took a meeting as a courtesy. They now know Bill and take his calls, since he made a good impression at the meeting.

BUDGET OPTIONS

The first time I went to AFM, my budget was almost non-existent. I took a Greyhound down from San Francisco, stayed at a hotel with a shared bathroom, and ate food from a nearby supermarket. I even took the bus to and from AFM.

If you have a car, it's not much more expensive or difficult to get to the airport hotels. They're a bit nicer and they don't require sharing a restroom. One year when I went to AFM, I stayed at a major chain near the airport. There were a fair amount of cheap restaurants nearby and the pool was cold but nice. However, you will need a car to stay near the airport.

AIRBNB

More than likely the best budget saver for AFM is AirBnB and other short term rental services. I've taken several more trips to LA since I wrote the first edition of this book and I've explored AirBnB quite thoroughly. I'll say that it's a very nice option for travelers on a budget.

I stayed at an AirBnB during AFM2015 and it was a very enjoyable experience. During my stay, the host had actually read the first edition of this book. She was courteous, had no problem picking up things while she was out, and always had a croissant waiting for me when I woke up. I could not have asked for a better experience.

Another trip in early 2016 was booked very last minute and I needed something for the next night. The only thing that was available in the area of Los Angeles that I needed to stay in was a shared room AirBnB. It was essentially a hostel near the Hollywood Walk of Fame. The host was great, but the girl staying in the bunk above me was not. I finished my work around 9PM, then I went out to explore the Walk of Fame because I had never been.

I had fun and took a picture next to David Bowie's star, almost bought a Selfie Stick but refrained, and then stopped for pizza and a pint at a Disney-themed bar. Once I mentioned I was a producer's rep to the bartender, he tried to pitch me on his "Avant-Garde" movie. I sat politely and watched a few scenes, and he comped my meal so I considered it fair.

Anyway, I got back to my AirBnB around midnight. I had to be up around 7AM for some very important meetings. I took a bit of time to get to sleep and around 2AM another set of people came in late and made a lot of noise getting in.

Again, It took me a whole to fall back asleep and then at 5AM I start to hear, "You've Lost that Loving Feeling" coming from the bunk above me. Apparently the girl in the bunk above me had her alarm set for 5AM and really likes to be ironic when she's staying in a hostel. Anyway, she silences it, then stays in bed. I try to grab a little bit of time and just about fall asleep again and then the song starts to play again. Again, she snoozes it. By the fifth time I hear the song, I've certainly lost the loving feeling and I'm starting to feel a very different feeling. It's sudden, new, and a little wicked. By about 6AM, a different alarm goes off and she gets up and gets ready for work. I'm awake so I just go to a coffee shop and start writing this edition, fully aware my editor will advise cutting this section. But I will fight for it. **[Editor's Note: I'm not being paid enough to fight you on this]**

So I had to attend five important meetings on far too little sleep. These included a powerful Sales Agent (who has contributed to this book), a former Principle at IMDb, and some pretty big producers who have done things you've heard of.

There are two morals to this story. First, if it's at all in the budget, get a private room. Second, if you can't, get some sleep aids. Additionally, AirBnB has some listings that are more business friendly. It's worth considering that filter when booking.

There is one other option that's worth mentioning. If you're going as a group, there are surprisingly affordable options for renting houses, condos, and apartments on AirBnB. This requires some more advanced planning, but it is a budget option that allows for much greater team-building.

If you are considering booking your lodging through AirBnb, check out the resource packet; there are some links and codes to save you some money for using AirBnB.

MINDSET

One thing to remember about AFM is that a good portion of success is mindset. It's an incredibly intense week where you'll be averaging 10-16 hour days filled with networking, meetings, and sales. Mindset is incredibly important. You'll be pushing yourself constantly with this schedule, so it's important your hotel feels like an escape. That will help you maintain your sanity while you work.

For that reason, make sure you choose a hotel for comfort – one you feel can be your home away from home. Also, make sure the commute isn't too long. You won't want to drive more than twenty minutes to get to your hotel after a long day – maybe thirty minutes with bad traffic. This puts the airport hotels just within range. It also makes getting to and from the airport and renting a car very easy.

The AFM hotels are very nice, but cost around $200 a night. While the comforts of a nice hotel can feel like a home away from home, the expense can be hard to manage. A rental car offers freedom, but the AFM shuttle system can get you all around Santa Monica without worries. If you must choose, make the choice that's best for you. Also consider that if you'll be getting around primarily on the shuttle, it makes parties easier and you won't have to worry if you have a drink to loosen up.

Really, it comes down to this: be safe, have fun, but remember you're there to work.

CHAPTER 5 – PROJECTS

Success at AFM can mean many things. If you have a completed project you're looking to sell, then your goal is to establish as much advance contact with sales agents and distributors as possible, set up meetings, and potentially even place your film before the market starts. As we mentioned in Chapter 1, it generally takes a few markets to start seeing revenue. Having your film placed before then can make a huge difference in how quickly you can sell your film. In order to do this the deal has to be finalized by mid-September at the latest.

If you can't quite get your film placed before the market, your goal is primarily to get as many screener requests as you can from sales agents while you're at the market. If you're lucky, you might get offered a deal memo during AFM. However you'll more than likely end up negotiating the deal during the week or two afterwards.

The first thing you need to consider when looking to go to the American Film Market is what projects you'll be pitching when you go. If you have a completed project seeking distribution, that's great. Your job will be a whole lot easier. If you don't have a completed project, that's fine, just make sure you have something to pitch.

DEVELOPMENT STAGE

If you're looking to get your project off the ground with no relationships, no track record, and no recognizable name talent attached, you're in for a rough road. It's nearly impossible to get a project that's still early in development off the ground with nothing but a script. Most sales agents or distributors just won't want to work with you if all you have is a script with no attachments. There's a certain amount of legwork that you, the producer, need to do before you can have a meeting with a sales agent that will actually lead to anything.

You need to figure out your target market. Part of that is a distributor or sales agent's job, but you need to be able to point them in the right direction. This book isn't about defining your target market, but it is something that filmmakers need to be aware of. There are many resources available on the subject, including some free information from the Film Insight Podcast I host. This subject is covered fairly thoroughly in Episode 2, with Prasenjit Chaudhuri.

A big thing you've got to keep in mind is that most of these sales agents are also filmmakers. If you come to them too early then they'll end up putting their own teams on the project. There's nothing wrong with that, and from their perspective it makes sense. They want to work with people they know and like because in the end, it's a safer investment for them. Building a business in film is heavily reliant on cultivated relationships and trust. This is true of building any business, but it's particularly true in the film business.

While the Film Industry is a creative industry, it is still an industry. In order for industry to properly function, it needs to be able to make a profit. These distributors and sales agents are putting a lot of money into any projects they take on, especially in the earlier stages of development so it's only logical that they would want to protect that investment by using people they know can get the job done.

If you come to them with a package that already has some attachments and a solid marketing plan you've got a much better shot at getting them on at an early stage. If you're coming to AFM at an early stage without a project that's at least near completion, then it's wise to have your goal at the market be to establish a relationship with several distributors and sales agents, rather than to sell them your in-development projects. The two go hand-in-hand and getting distributors and sales agents interested requires a little of both.

BRING THREE PROJECTS

Generally, if you're still in the script/concept stage, I recommend you have three projects in development you're seeking distribution for. This is due primarily to the fact that not every buyer you'll talk to will be interested in all the projects you're selling. If this is your first film, you are a lot more likely to see success if you focus on making genre pictures.

Opinions vary about the wisdom of splitting focus, but the advantage of bringing three films is that generally a buyer is looking for something very specific, and if he doesn't like your lead pitch, their next question is going to be something along the lines of, "What else you got?" If you've brought three projects, you can launch immediately into your next pitch. I have personally found success doing this. You'll be much more likely to turn that person you're talking to from a card in your file to a contact who will take your call. You'll also want to make sure you have information on each project you're pitching that distributors or sales agents can take with them.

I know this contradicts some of the advice listed previously in this chapter, but even if you don't have that much in place for these projects, bring what you have. It can open doors and start a conversation with a sales agent you can follow up with at a later date. The market is very much about relationships. In order to build professional relationships, you need to be able to talk business at the drop of a hat. If all you've got is a postcard, you're unlikely to find much success in garnering financing, but it's possible you can establish a relationship and get a letter of intent.

In fact, you'll have a lot more success if all you're looking for at AFM is a letter of intent to take to outside investors. It doesn't get you the money you need to get the film made, but it gets you a whole lot closer. Also, most sales agents will never be the first money in. If they put any money in before the film is completed, it will likely come in the form of a Minimum Guarantee (MG) you can then take to a bank and get a secured loan based on that contract. However it should be noted not all sales agents are reliable enough for a bank to make a loan based on an MG. Additionally, you'll need to budget for interest payments which can sometimes be quite substantial. Sites like Slated can help with relatively low-interest secured debt financing, often at a lower rate or with fewer requirements than a bank.

If you are at an early stage, then the best thing you can do is to focus on building relationships with distributors and sales agents. Cultivating relationships is the only way to build a business in the film industry because of how much success in the industry relies on social currency and political capital.

FOCUS ON GENRE PICTURES

Filmmakers often underestimate the importance of genre in selling a motion picture. It's actually one of the most important things international buyers and sales agents focus on when buying a film. There's a reason for this. The genre is a good indicator as to who will be interested in it.

Focusing on genre is particularly important for international sales. International sales are an increasingly important part of the independent film distribution game, and how well a film sells internationally is highly dependent on the genre in which the sales agent positions it.

There are certain genres that sell better than others. Until recently, the really hot sellers at AFM were action, horror, and thriller. But family movies are making a comeback in a really big way. There's a big demand right now that's not being filled at the moment for family pictures. A lot of buyers only deal in completed projects, but there's such a gap in the demand that family pictures are getting presales on a far more regular basis than has been recently seen.

As of the publication of the second edition, family is going strong and horror has waned a bit. Action and thriller are still strong.

Just as there are genres that should be focused on for greater profitability, there are also genres that should be avoided. Generally countries don't import dramas. There's a lot of money to be made on dramas in the country of origin, but since international sales often accounts for as much as 70% of a film's total revenue, it's generally unwise to position it as a drama. That said, a good drama can be positioned in another way to help it sell internationally.

Dialogue-heavy comedies are often difficult to sell internationally, due to the language barrier. If the film is made for under five million dollars and doesn't have some damn near A-list names in it, it often doesn't make financial sense to dub or subtitle the film. Comedies in general are a bit of a difficult sell on an international basis as well, due to the fact that humor varies so greatly from culture to culture.

In order to drive this point home, just think about the different roles of women in the real life cultures of America and most of Western Europe versus those in the Middle East. Repeat the same question for LGBT people. Now think about the dynamics of dating in San Francisco and Utah.

There's a great film example of this that I learned in Film School. *American Pie* is one of not a huge amount of comedies to do quite well internationally. Part of it was the fact that there's a lot of pretty people and debauchery in the film, but not all of it. A larger part is that they had a lot of different types of humor in the film.

For example, in the infamous pie scene, Americans laugh at Jason Biggs doing terrible things to the pie. Europeans laugh when the parents walk in and at the following conversation.

Don't mix genres if you can avoid it, although if you can define your genre a little more it can be helpful. One of my projects that garnered a lot of interest was a psychosexual thriller that my former production company was producing. An action/drama doesn't sell to both people who like action movies and people who like dramas; it sells only to people who like both of those genres. At least that's what most sales agents will tell you if you take the time to ask. In fact, I've had sales agents tell me this verbatim and have then stayed up all night to rewrite entire treatments in verbiage that emphasize action over drama.

I'm not saying you should make a cookie cutter horror movie. There needs to be some element of originality in what you're doing, or no one will be interested. What I am suggesting is that you tell a story you're passionate about, but try to come up with one in a genre people have heard of and tends to be popular.

IF IT'S YOUR FIRST FEATURE

If you've not made a film before, you have to understand that buyers are looking for certain things. If you want to make a sustainable career out of filmmaking you'll have to understand that the only real way to do that is to make films that turn a profit. On the ultra-low-budget scale, genre pictures are one of the most viable ways to give yourself the best chance to make money with your film. Horror has been the best to help launch your career, but it's currently unclear as to how long that will remain true.

A sales agent I met at AFM once told me that the things distributors and buyers are looking for are movies with girls and guns. They're looking for these because they're the movies that sell well overseas, as well as selling to larger retail outlets domestically. The same sales agent also told me that the most important thing when making your first film is to make something you're passionate about. I agree with him on both these points. The old adage "sex sells" is just as true as ever, but making a film is a labor-intensive process that's a lot of hard work for very little monetary compensation when you're starting out.

If you're not passionate about the film you're making, there's a much higher chance it will never be completed. If your film is never completed, there's absolutely no way it will ever make money. Your first project doesn't need to be perfect, but it does need to get done and it needs to be good.

That said, passion is not the most important thing in making a movie. It is important, but there are a lot of people passionate about their projects. It is basically a baseline minimum you need to have, but not something that will impress a distributor or sales agent. Everyone is passionate about filmmaking; that's why we do it. You need to be able to articulate why your story needs to be told and why it will make money. This requires thorough market research.

If it's your first feature, you may well be better off just making it happen than trying to get investment. Make a low-budget genre picture with your friends on the weekends. Spend as little as you can on it, but make it good. It's more possible now than ever to shoot a film with little money. Once it's completed, take it to AFM and talk to sales agents. You probably won't make much money with it, but you'll be a far more proven entity. Don't just hack it together. You've got to make it good and make sure that your deliverables are up to par. If you've gone to film school, do things by the book, but make a film that costs as little as possible. You still won't make money until you sell the film, but if you make it for cheap there's less to recoup. If you make a film for very little money, that may enable you to recoup more than your investment.

Dov Simmens said, "Make it one location, with no props". That advice was good enough to launch Quentin Tarantino's career. If you follow it and bring a completed project to AFM you'll be in a much better position than you will with a briefcase full of scripts, a heart full of passion, and a head full of dreams.

Filmmakers are storytellers, so if there is a story you need to tell, write it and pitch it. If you're still in development, see if you can bring a story to life that falls within one of the hot genres. If it's not in one of the hot genres, you may be better served by putting that project on hold and going back to the drawing board to come up with something that is. Don't forget about that story; just come back to it once you've made another project so that you've got a proven track record.

BUDGET

Another thing that you need to keep in mind about AFM is that it is the realm of truly independent film. Most films at AFM will probably never see a US theatrical release. If they do, it will be limited, barring extraordinary circumstances, of course. The giant blockbusters don't generally tend to show at AFM. So when you're pitching a film at AFM, try to keep the budget realistic. With some exceptions, most AFM success stories are for films budgeted under three million dollars. Opinions on this vary, but generally budgets under one million are preferred. Up to five million is possible, assuming you've completed a film before and have a couple attachments.

There are some commonly accepted numbers that vary a bit year to year, but in order to stand the best chance at profitability a film must be budgeted under 1 million or over 10 million dollars.

My best advice to you is that if you're making your first feature, keep it under $200,000. Honestly, lower is better. If it's your first and you can do it for $65,000, do it for that. It's far easier to sell a completed film than one in development. That said, there does need to be a certain level of quality for you to get distributed. If it's not good, no one can sell it in a meaningful way.

You must make sure your deliverables are up to par. If they're not, you won't get any money for your project. Get a friend in film school to help you edit over the summer. Make sure that he understands the importance of a professional workflow. This is truer now than ever. Although there are new platforms seeking new content, everyone is looking for a good-looking, good-sounding film that was well written.

It is wise to get your first feature in the can by any means necessary, but there is one exception worth paying for. That exception is recognizable and marketable name talent. If it is possible to get more recognized name talent in your film if you raise the budget a small amount, do it.

Another very important thing to focus on if you take the uber-independent route is making your film in a marketable genre.

If you've got a drama or a comedy, cast is incredibly important. It's nearly impossible to sell either of those genres without known talent, or at least some festival success. Even with both those in place, it can often be a losing battle.

Shortly before this edition was published, AFM released some excellent statistics regarding what films "break out". What constitutes a breakout film? AFM defined it as a film from a first time director, budgeted between 500K and 3mm USD that grossed more than 10mm at the box office. According to those statistics, the best chance you have at making a breakout film is to make a drama.

However, it's important to keep in mind that according to their own statistics, only four films break out in a year, on average. While exact statistics as to how many feature films are made in a year are difficult to find, the best estimates I've been able to find put that number somewhere between 5,000 and 10,000.

Additionally, dramas are not the only genre to break out. While their statistics just had high quality, well produced dramas as the most likely films to break out, they only accounted for about 50% of total breakouts in the study. Many of their examples also had somewhat notable cast or producers attached. Many also had some involvement from some sort of lab, similar to Sundance labs.

Thriller and horror films were also on the breakout list. And even if they don't break out, they're much easier to sell so you can recoup at least some of your investment. Sure, it's moderately less likely your film will break out, but the horror and thriller films that do break out tend to do so in a huge way. The Blair Witch Project, Insidious, and The Devil Inside stand out as examples. Granted, neither The Blair Witch Project nor Insidious would meet AFM's criteria due to their low budgets, but their ROIs were just astounding.

So, if you happen to be able to put together an extremely high quality film with some talent attached, and can weather the risk of not being able to make a dime on it, make a drama. If you want to start a career in film, with a chance to break out and a much higher likelihood of making a decent return even if you don't break out, then make a genre picture.

Another thing to keep in mind is that films do have a shelf life and if you don't sell your film within a year or so of completion, it's really difficult to get any distribution for it. There comes a point where your goal is not just to make money, but also to get bigger exposure for your next film. Always make money where possible, but it's not always possible. If that's the case, the next priority is getting it seen. There's a lot more on this in the final section of the book.

While a lot of this chapter has been focused on making a film for as little as possible, it's also important to note that while cutting costs is important, the most important thing to focus on is how you're going to get money coming back in. Have a distribution and marketing plan. Learn about how you'll monetize your feature. A friend once told me that marketing is like shooting an arrow and market research is like placing a target. Distributors and sales agents are good marketers, but you need to help them place the target.

In the end, the most important thing to focus on is how you're going to make money and see revenue back. Part of that is closely controlling costs and part of that is having a plan for revenue. The latter is more important.

A NOTE ON COMPLETED PROJECTS

If you do have a completed or near-completed film, it would behoove you to attend the market that's closest to when you complete the film. Films are not evergreen. They do not last forever. About a year or two after the initial release the value of the film drops drastically.

So if you're submitting your film to festivals, then it's probably good enough to submit to sales agents. Although you should be aware, no sales agent will watch a movie more than once. Don't rush your film just to make AFM, because in many ways it's better if it's completed the next year.

CHAPTER 6 – Prepared Documents

Now that you've booked your badge and hotel and figured out what projects you're going to be bringing to the AFM, it's time to get the things you'll need for pitching at AFM in order. This step should be done about 2 or 3 weeks before you leave for the market, as a lot may change in the time leading up to the market, and you want your printed materials to be as up to date as possible. You will need those two or three weeks to ensure your printed materials will get to you in time. For easy reference, here's a loosely prioritized list of what you need.

In reality, while you should have all of these documents prepared, the most important by far are the top 3-4. In order to save on your budget, you may want to give much of numbers 5 and 6 a miss on printing. This has been modified from the first edition in order to better show what you should have printed and have available electronically.

Priority	Physical	Electronic
1	Business Cards	
2		-Website
3.	Postcards Trailer DVDs DVD Screeners	Electronic Press kit
4.	Press kit	
5.	**Meetings Only** Treatments Executive Summaries Topsheet Budgets	
6.		Marketing Plans

BUSINESS CARDS

The first and most important thing you can bring to the American Film Market is your business card. Nobody is going to take you seriously if you don't have one. Really, you should carry them with you wherever you go. I've picked up clients in line at the local coffee shop, and investors singing karaoke in a gay bar.

I recommend you get standard 2 inches by 3.5 inches business cards. The small business cards are easy to lose and I generally don't like getting them. Have your business cards custom designed with your logo. Make sure they have your name, company, position, phone, and email.

Cards aren't that expensive, especially if you use one of many online providers. That said, make sure you spend enough money that only your branding is on the card. Certain free providers include the printer's branding on them. They feel cheap. Even if you don't have money, you don't want to let people know you don't have money. It's generally very little extra to have a card that has a blank back as opposed to someone else's branding.

I've done a fair amount of research, and generally I've found that, as of this publishing date, GotPrint.com has the best prices on printing, with very few add-ons for things like file upload.

If you have the choice between no card and a stock card from one of the major printers, then the major printer's card is definitely the way to go. If you have the money, you can hire a freelancer to design your cards for you. It's generally not that expensive from a provider like elance.com. If you've already have a logo you can get a card done for as little as $50 on UpWork, and you might even be able to find one for 5 bucks on Fiverr. They're often surprisingly well done for the price point.

Regarding logo, don't underestimate the importance of your company's brand. If you went to film school, you probably have a decent familiarity with Photoshop, or at least know people who do. Your corporate logo should be simple, eye catching and memorable. Gary Tomchuk, a long time Silicon Valley strategist who's helped to launch dozens of companies, gave me the following advice: When designing a logo, think about how it would look in the corner of the screen as you watch television. The major network logos are simple and recognizable from a thumbnail. Yours should be, too.

This is another thing you can go to Fiverr to, if you need to get it done on the cheap. I've done it before, and was pleasantly surprised by quality.

Your card is a stand-in for you, so it is very important you get it right. If you have more than one member of your production company attending, it is advisable that you all have cards on the same template, with the same logo, as it will make you look more cohesive and like you're a larger company.

If you're attending AFM as a couple, or as several people in the same company, it is still advisable you each have individual cards. They're not that expensive, and there's always a little bit of a weird vibe if you give away someone else's card.

 Personally, I favor a thicker card stock, as it still falls within the realm of acceptable card size but makes your card stand out a bit more and subconsciously can make your company feel a bit more substantial and stable. Generally a very good thing to convey when you want to do business with people.

There is one drawback to thick cards. If the person you're meeting has a filing system of using the standard business card pages, the thicker cards may not fit. This may cause your card to just get thrown out because they don't want to deal with cutting it down in order to keep it. It's best to find a healthy balance and use a thick card stock, but not the thickest card stock that's available.

WEBSITE

As the world moves ever more increasingly online, a website for your production company and your film becomes increasingly important. Being on the web increases your credibility, and gives people you meet a good place to find you online and can actually help bring in a bit of business. I get the vast majority of my business through my website, with some coming through my social media presence.

Your can also be a great place to host all of your projects, and a single URL where people can find all of your social media and everything about you on the web.

They also don't need to be difficult to build. I'm an executive at 3 different organizations, and each has a website I help to administer. I'm currently an Admin for a Weebly site, a Wordpress Site, and a Drupal Site. Only one I completely built myself, and that's the Weebly one, which is theguerrillarep.com. It's a very easy to use WYSIWYG [What you see is what you get] website editor.

It's worth paying a bit more to get your own domain. I know I always snark a bit about people who use the something akin to companyname.weebly.com. The service plan and domain aren't that expensive, and if you enable google adsense, you can even make enough money from ads on your site that it ends up free. That's what I do.

DOMAINS AND EMAIL ADDRESSES

Another thing that a website allows is a custom email address. Having an email address that is YourName@YourCompany.com is much better than having an email that is Your.Name123@majorprovider.com, or yourproject.themovie@majorprovider.com. That said, either of those are better than SuperHotBabe@majorprovider.com, or something equivalently silly. Keep in mind this is a professional event, and people will judge you based on your card and email address.

Having an email that's easy to write down and remember is also a very good thing. If your email is BobbyJ_K_2113@this-movie-title-is-super-long-and-hard-to-remember.com or something along those lines, then it will be hard to say it on the phone, and harder for them to take down in follow-up. I would not recommend using such an email.

PROJECT CARDS

The second thing you need is representation for your projects. Before I go into the specific printables you'll need, I'm going to take a moment to say what really sells your film.

One of the most important things you can spend time and money on is developing a good poster. There was once a time where you could sell a movie with a good pitch and a good poster alone. That's much less true than it used to but that's not to undersell the importance of a solid postcard. The other most important part of selling a film is a good trailer. To a certain degree, a good poster and a good trailer have more influence on selling your film than your film does.

This is not the be all and end all of the sales process. The quality of your film is and always will be very important. However filmmakers often underestimate the importance of a good trailer and poster in selling film. The big reason for this, especially in the realm of Video on Demand (V.O.D.) distribution, is the consumer will often only watch the trailer and read the tagline and synopsis before deciding whether or not to purchase the film.

If the film is being watched on an SVOD platform like Netflix, Amazon Prime, or HBO Go, they're likely to make a decision of whether or not to spend the time watching the film based on the poster, synopsis, and trailer. Buyers for these platforms have taken notice of this, and are making purchase decisions based on the quality of the poster and trailer. Often even more so than the film.

While postcards are pretty much ideal for giving a good view of the good sized reminder of your onesheet while allowing for short synopsis on the back, AFM security will stop you if you try to hand them out. It's against the rules to hand them out in the lobby if you're not an exhibitor. You can't hand out anything bigger than a business card. If you have the budget, getting a few postcards is helpful for your exhibitor meetings.

There was one time I tried to have individual project business cards. It was meant as a solution to AFM Blue-Badged Security not allowing people to give out anything bigger than a business card. They had the onesheet on one side, and the genre, tagline, website, and your contact information on the other. I had 5 cards that year, and saw limited success, although the films weren't that good. Although honestly, I think there are better solutions like excessive amounts of advance contact.

IF YOUR FILM IS COMPLETED

If your film is completed, make sure you bring screeners, but be careful whom you give them to. There are pirates who attend AFM, and you don't want your content stolen. If you have a meeting with an IFTA Member, it's generally fine to give them a screener. If they have a red attendee badge, even if they talk big it's generally not advisable to give them a screener. Although, if you can take the time to do some due diligence on them, then it may be reasonable to give them a screener.

There is some wiggle room in this, but you have to remember that there are pirates out there.

You probably don't need your budget if your film is completed. You should still have your business plan and marketing plan, especially the parts where you show your target demographic and how you plan to access it. It's good to let the sales agent know you've thought about these things. If you haven't, you should. It's never too early to consider what your target demographics, even if you're still in the script stage.

SCREENERS

For your screener, don't make the menu overly complicated. Make sure you include the full cut of the movie on it, and if you have a trailer make sure that's there too. And make sure you put your contact information on the disk. It's easy for contact details to get lost, so having it directly on the disk makes it so as long as they have the movie, they have your details. That said, put your contact details on the case as well, it's hard to have it in too many places when you're giving a screener to a sales agent or distributor.

Also, it might not be a bad idea to put your copyright registration number on the case. It both helps dissuade pirates from stealing your movie, and also helps show sales agents and distributors that your chain of title documents are probably in order.

I would think this goes without saying, but make sure you've registered your film for copyright through copyright.gov. If you don't, it's easy for others to steal it and cut you out of the loop on your own movie. It is not expensive; so make sure you do it before AFM. The same goes for your script. Don't just register it with the WGA. Copyright it as well. They're different and you need both.

EPK

An EPK is an electronic press kit that has some artwork from your film, and a few clippings regarding any reviews, information on any festivals and awards the film has received, links and questions from any press coverage for the film, and some information on any notable talent and key crew members. You can find advice for making your press kit online.

The reason you want to have an electronic press kit is that it can be quite expensive to get them printed at any sufficient quality.

You probably also won't need enough of them to justify printing them at a high enough quality to give them away as widely as you would need to.

TRAILER DVDS

It's good to have these for easy access to your films' promotional materials. If you've got a screener and only have one movie you're selling, then just include it on the screener. Make sure it looks really good. If you've shot a finance trailer, it has to be fantastic for it to get any traction.

Although, I will say that I have yet to see any success from finance trailers.

MEETING PRINTABLES

If you get meetings at AFM, there are certain things you're going to want to have at the ready for the sales agent or distributor. You'll need a one-page treatment for each project, and it is advisable that you bring a couple executive summaries for all your projects as well. I favor a onesheet that has all three projects and your website on it for inclusion in any meeting. I've found the best way to organize all of this is with a meeting folder. Personally, I even go ahead and brand my folders for organization; that keeps the sales agent thinking about you and your brand. This is another one of those tricks that isn't that expensive but makes your company look bigger and more distinguished, even if you're just starting out.

Many filmmakers simply don't think about their company's brand. Demonstrating you've thought about yours puts you above the crowd of people who just walk into AFM. It shows you have a greater understanding of marketing, which looks good to a distributor. I do it with some simple three by five inch stickers printed in black that I attach to folders. You can also have your folders embossed at major office supply stores, but that can get expensive.

That said, these are far from a necessity, even when they do look good, what you really need to be doing is building relationships, not simply making great printables. While the quality of your printed materials can give a great first impression, it's far from the most important thing you can do with your money.

TREATMENTS

Make sure to clearly define your movie in your treatment. Keep in mind this is a sales based treatment, not simply something to tell people about your movie. Selling a story and telling a story are related, but different skills. Be as succinct as possible, while hitting the selling points of the film. You'll find more information on that in the next chapter.

EXECUTIVE SUMMARIES

Regarding the executive summary, it's good to have revenue projections, but honestly all it really does is show you've done your homework. The sales agent is going to know their market a whole lot better than you will, and they're going to base their assumptions on their experience more than on your numbers. If you're in early stages of a project revenue projections may be better left out.

Don't be too attached to your numbers, because they're not going to be a huge selling point to these sales agents or distributors. In fact, you may want to leave them out for market meetings. Sales agents and distributors have access to information the rest of us don't, and decades of experience.

It's still good to take the time to make the projections and comparables, so that you know what the market is like for your film. When you talk to a distributor or sales agent pulling out other similar films that have done well at the box office looks like you did your homework, but this is something that you will need some experience in to do well.

BUDGET

Don't include more than a topsheet budget. If you include a detail budget, it opens up the ability for the person you're meeting with to go through it with a fine tooth comb and point out anything for which you've over or under budgeted. That's never a good way for a conversation to go.

While this isn't a book on budgeting, one thing film schools don't teach well is that you need to allocate money for promotion, festival travel, and market travel. Don't overlook this expense, as it makes a huge difference in how much your film will return to investors, and showing you've accounted for it puts a distributor's mind at ease.

You don't have to budget for all of the promotional expenses it, but allocating money for it is wise. Although, this may be something you'll want to put in a separate budget. If you include them in your standard budget, then that may put you into a higher bracket for the guilds. That up in budget tier can cause your expenses to rise very quickly.

It may be a better idea to raise promotional funds as the film is reaching completion to avoid the bump in union tier. This is also the easiest time to raise money. Although you should let your investors know this is your intent early on.

MARKETING PLAN

The most important thing about your marketing plan is defining your target market. This requires market research.

A good friend of mine, Sheridan Tatsuno, (another long time Silicon Valley strategist,) defined market research as finding the target, and marketing as shooting the arrow. It's a very apt metaphor, and if we extend it, the distributor/sales agent is an excellent archer skilled at hitting a target, but in order for them to properly do it you must first point them in the right direction so they know what they're aiming at.

It is wise to develop a marketing plan for each project, at the very least, if not a full business plan.

BUSINESS PLAN

If you have a full business plan, bring a few copies of it. This is probably the lowest on your priorities list. Speaking from experience, they cost 20-30 bucks each to print, and generally not many people will ask to see them.

The best way to learn how to write a business plan is through the book *Filmmakers and Financing* by Louise Levison. It is the standard for film industry business plans. There's also *The Independent Filmmakers Guide to Writing a Business Plan for Investors*, by Gabriel Campisi. These are both books every producer should read.

There are also places you can take classes on writing business plans. The Producer Foundry will be offering classes on the subject that will greatly assist in preparing you to write a competent business plan. Check the resource packet discounts and additional information on the current classes available through Producer Foundry.

CHAPTER 7 – PITCHES

Now that you've got your printed materials all sorted, you're going to want to get your pitch down pat. You'll want to have a ten-second version and a thirty-second version. Your ten-second version is more important than your thirty-second version. If you don't have them in the first ten seconds, they'll be gone before you count to thirty. Knowing when you've lost the interest of the person you're pitching to is a skill that comes with time, although there are indicators we'll cover in the "Lobby" section.

Don't expect to get your pitches right the first time through. You'll need to spend a few hours refining them and making them punchy. You'll need a 10 second high concept pitch for each of the projects you've brought to AFM. Your pitch should include the following.

1. The genre

2. The status of the film (script, funded, in post, completed, etc)

3. What stars you have (if any)

4. One sentence overview of the plot.

5. The budget range

It may sound a little formulaic, but you've got to keep in mind most of the people you really want to talk to hear dozens if not hundreds of these a day at AFM and don't want to have their time wasted with what they deem unnecessary information. All of the buyers and sales agents there will understand their markets a whole lot better than you will. While it's not something that you should ever say outright, passion for your project will go a long way towards selling it.

This will be covered more thoroughly in the lobby section, but never just start pitching to someone without opening up a conversation with him or her first. It's rude, and quickly wears on people's nerves.

GENRE

The reason you start with the genre is it's probably the biggest factor in selling a film at the AFM. You can't dawdle on the genre, and the piece needs to have a clear and strong genre if it's to find a footing in the marketplace. Even if you haven't created a piece in one of the AFM hot genres (horror, action, thriller, and recently, family,) you need to be clear on what your genre is, and say it right away.

STATUS

For the status, if the film is in development, you can leave this out. If it's in post, you can leave it for follow up conversation shortly after the pitch. If it's completed, that should be one of the first things you say. Completed films are easier to sell. Most times people will request a screener if they're at all interested in your film. If they request it, hand it to them immediately. If they don't, ask if they'd like one.

TALENT

Talent is a huge part of selling a film, and if you have a recognizable name or face attached you should make sure you mention it every time. If you do have talent, don't overstate their involvement. Don't tell a sales agent they're in the movie for twenty minutes if they're only in it for five, and make sure whatever talent you have has given you permission to use their name in marketing.

Most times if they've signed onto your film, they will have no problem with you using their name to market it, but with bigger talent can sometimes come restrictions on how you use the name in terms of billing. If they're only in the movie for five minutes, you may need to use something like "featuring" "big action star" instead of, "starring" "big action star."

STORY

The most important thing to remember about a pitch is that you're not telling your story; you're selling your story. Take some time to figure out how to sell your story, and work with your friends to get it punchy. You can also read the backs of DVD covers so you get an idea of what makes a good story pitch.

Little differences in how you say something can make all the difference at AFM. If you try to sell a movie by saying "it's a thriller about a couple of lesbians as they fall in love, lose innocence and experiment with drugs. Then one of them goes back to dating men and the other is heartbroken.," They'll be gone before you hit your second sentence.

If, on the other hand, you sell that same movie by saying, "it's a psychosexual thriller, and a story of drugs, desire, and dangerous obsession; Blair and Nikki fall into a whirlwind romance, and are lead down a path of destruction," you'll get a lot more attention.

Focus on the action of the story, keep it short, and above all emphasize the conflict. Storytelling 101 in film school is always that there is no drama and no interest without conflict. The same should be in your pitches. You have to hook them in less than 10 seconds while summarizing an entire 90-minute story. It's a daunting task, but it's something that can be mastered with the help of friends, business partners, and above all, practice.

Another thing that's really useful is naming your characters. There's a certain level of emotional attachment we hear from just a name. If all I hear are a couple of lesbians that's one thing. If I hear Blair and Nikki I'm more interested.

Also, don't give up the ghost. It's better to leave them wondering what happens so they actually want to watch the film.

BUDGET RANGE

You never want to give the exact budget of the film, but you do need to give a rough idea of what it cost to make it. Generally, the ranges you'll mention are under $200,000, between $200,000 and $500,000, between $500,000 and one million, between one and three million, between three and five million, and between five and ten million.

The reason you don't want to give the exact budget is that the budget of the film strongly affects the sales price. Some sales agents make their calculations for the price range of how they'll sell your film based on the budget you give them. You can really shoot yourself in the foot by saying how much you spent. If you've made your movie well, if it's beautiful and sounds good, a buyer might think you spent more on it, which means a better deal for you.

Now, if you've spent more than five million dollars on your movie, I'm surprised you're reading this book. That level of budget should have had some money set aside for prints and advertising, and attracting a sales agent should have been a easier, and probably necessary in order to raise your budget.

Generally budgets are broken into ranges. I usually use the SAG agreements as benchmarks, but I add one for micro budget features. If it's under $50,000, it's micro budget. If it's between $50,000 and $200,000, it's ultra low. If it's between $200,000 and $900,000, it's modified low budget. If it's between $900,000 and two and a half million, it's low budget.

At somewhere like AFM, these numbers are highly variable and often tend more towards the low end of the scale, but that's the guideline I go by. Only use one of the two descriptors for budget range, and just go with whatever feels natural to you in the pitch. They vary slightly, but both should translate.

For example, I'd say that a film budgeted under one million dollars is low, between one and three million is medium, and above that I'd just say what the budget was.

PASSION

Getting together with friends to work on pitches can be quite fun. A friend of mine once told me that "everything in business is theater." What he meant was that the way people present themselves is all about cultivating an image and making a strong and memorable impression. This is especially true in show business. You're not selling paper products, financial services, or insurance; you're selling entertainment. Make your pitch entertaining. Tell a story, captivate your audience, emphasize the drama.

When you're passionate about what you're selling it will come through in your pitch. If you're not, you're in the wrong business. If you have already completed the film you may well be coming up with what Daniel Riviera, an entertainment transactional attorney based in San Francisco, calls "Producer Burnout." In his interview on the Film Insight Podcast, Mr. Riviera said, "The number 1 Distribution Gotcha is Producer Burnout. You're just so exhausted from physically getting the film made, raising the money, getting past all the other challenges that arise that you're burned out. You need to regroup. Preparing for this next phase is another challenge."

Staying passionate about something for such a long time can be a tricky task, but you need to show your passion when you are pitching. Perhaps showing that passion is as simple as remembering why you made the film in the first place. If you can show a distributor or a sales agent that passion, then they'll be more interested in working with you.

Again, it's not the be-all-end-all, but it is a requirement that you be passionate about the film. Don't ever say you're passionate about it; let the drive come through in how you pitch. If you have to say you are passionate about it, they'll probably turn you down, because you shouldn't need to say it.

The ability to pitch well comes with practice, but you should be able to pull out your pitch at the drop of a hat. Ask some friends to randomly quiz you on the pitch in the weeks leading up to AFM. If you're going with a group, quiz them randomly when you see them. It needs to be ingrained in your head so well that you can pull it out any time without thinking about it. The last thing you want to be doing is trying to remember your pitch when you meet someone; it will sound canned and no one really cares. Know your pitch well enough that you can let the passion for your project speak for itself.

CHAPTER 8 – RESEARCH/ADVANCE CONTACT

Doing your research is paramount. It really can make the difference between having great success and having no success. Not every sales agent is right for a film, and finding the right sales agent is key to maximizing your returns. Understanding what sorts of films a sales agent works with will save you time, increase your likelihood of success, and enable you to get the best deal possible for your film. In fact, as you'll read in Chapter 23, doing your research was the number one piece of advice that all respondents gave.

Not all sales agents are the same. As stated in the prologue, the business of international sales is one that relies heavily on relationships. Sales agents spend decades cultivating strong relationships across with buyers from across the globe.

Each sales agent has strong relationships with different buyers, who specialize in different sorts of projects. It's important to know what sorts of relationships that sales agent is likely to have when approaching them in advance.

Once you buy your AFM badge, you'll be granted access to MyAFM. On MyAFM, there is a list of all the exhibitors attending AFM. You can look at their profiles to find everything you'll need to know about them. The Primary information you'll want to know is listed below, as well as a brief description of why you'll want to know that information. Access to MyAFM is the biggest reason you should buy your badge early. Here's that list of information you'll want.

1. The budget range they work in

2. The genres they work in

3. Their market lineup

4. Films they've distributed in the past.

5. The first and last name of their acquisitions lead.

BUDGET RANGE

These are mostly the same budget ranges mentioned in the last section, under 500K, 500K to one million, one million to three million, three million to five million, five million to ten million, ten million to twenty million, and over twenty million. There will be occasions when distributors will pick up the projects for over twenty million, but the vast majority of filmmakers will never reach that level, particularly as budgets continually drop with new technology. If it's your first film you'll want to focus on the lower end. In my opinion, a good range to shoot for is about $200K.

It's an entirely different skill to sell a film budgeted at $100K than it is to sell one budgeted at ten million dollars. Marketing techniques for different budget ranges varies greatly, as do the revenue structures. Distributors and sales agents tend to specialize in certain ranges, and have become experts at making money for those ranges. In all industries, a huge part of marketing is price. Having a sales agent who sells $100K films sell your $10mm film would be like trying to sell Armani at K-Mart.

When you log on to MyAFM, the budget ranges a sales agent works with are listed right on the sidebar. You can also look up a sales agent on IMDbPro and take a look at the films they've helped to distribute, then access the budget from the Business section. Not all budgets are listed there, but a lot of them are. IMDbPro is a paid service, but it's an invaluable tool to the independent filmmaker. Apart from this research, it allows you access to phone numbers and emails for all agents and many distributors, making contact far easier. You can get a 14-day free trial and compress your research if necessary.

GENRE

As mentioned previously, genre is one of the biggest pieces in selling a film at a market like AFM. AFM is unofficially known as the home of the genre piece. This is admittedly less true than it was in previous years, but it is still a very important part of selling any film.

The way genres sell in each territory varies greatly, so sales agents often specialize in one genre or another. They'll be more likely to pick up one film or another based on the genres they typically work in. The most important asset of any sales agent is the relationship they've cultivated with buyers, and often buyers will come to them looking for a specific type of movie from those sales agents. However this is not always the case.

Some sales agents will switch the genre they work in with very little notice. There are several who have specialized in one genre for decades, and as the market shifted they completely switched focus to an entirely different Genre. One of the best examples of this I've heard was a sales agents who switched from selling almost exclusively horror films to children's and family movies (you should be sensing a trend here, but remember how quickly trends change). They transitioned on it in only about a year, and shifted their entire catalog with it.

Most of the reputable sales agents you would work with at the market will have a good idea on how to sell most genres. However, they have much better skill set for selling the particular genres they've developed their brand around. Just as you should develop a style and brand as a filmmaker, distributors and sales agents develop a voice and a brand for the types of projects they produce. It really is best to target the sales agents and distributors who have slates with movies similar to your own. This segues nicely into . . .

MARKET LINEUP

An exhibitor's market lineup is the slate they're selling at that particular market. It will give you a really good idea of the types of films they sell, and you'll want to list the ones similar to your projects. Make sure to write down those that are similar to yours so you can reference them when you're trying to get a meeting. You can find this information on MyAFM.

If you have a horror film budgeted at $120K and they've got a few of those featured on their slate, then it's a good bet you should talk to them. If they focus on all horror, then that's a good bet as well. One sales agent who goes there has made their name in martial arts movies, and sells the Chuck Norris Catalog. Finding sales agents and distributors with similar slates to yours will greatly increase your chances for success at AFM.

FILMS THEY HAVE DISTRIBUTED BEFORE

Similarly, the films they've distributed in the past are also important to consider. However since sometimes a distributor or sales agent will change the sorts of films they work with, it's less important than their current market lineup. Knowing how long they've been dealing with films similar to yours is good information, which can help you figure out how much experience they have in your genre.

How different genres are doing at any point changes fairly rapidly, as does the market for independent film. Because of this, anything older than about five years doesn't have too much bearing on the current market. Keeping that in mind, it does little good to reference a film the sales agent worked with ten years ago as a reason they should distribute yours. Unless it was far and away their biggest success, odds are you'll do better referencing films that are much more recent. This is because it's a much better indication of what is currently selling, and where their interests currently lie. It's also a good indication of the direction they're taking their brand.

NAME OF THEIR ACQUISITIONS LEAD

This is quite possibly the most important piece of information you'll research and write down. I've mentioned before, little changes in approach can make all the difference in whether or not you make a sale, or even get a meeting. If you go in and ask for their acquisitions lead by name you'll be in a far better position than if you simply ask for whoever is in charge of acquisitions.

I cannot stress this enough; it pays to do your homework. I've done it both ways, and it's always better to know the head of their acquisitions person. A big part of the job in getting meetings is getting past the assistant. These people talk to dozens of filmmakers a day while at the market, and their job is to weed out the meetings that won't be productive. If you go in and ask for a meeting by that person by name, then you'll be far more likely to make a meeting.

PRIORITIZING YOUR CONTACT

When preparing to contact sales agents in advance, you should prioritize who you want to reach out to.

My advice is to make 3 tiers, each with 5 contacts in them. Reach out to the first tier about 6-8 weeks before AFM, the second about 4-6 weeks, and the final tier 2-4 weeks out.

The first tier should be your ideal distribution companies. The biggest and most reputable companies that will take your project the farthest. Your non-filmmaker friends might have even heard of some of their projects.

The second tier would be slightly smaller companies, but still ones that can take your projects and get them fairly wide scale distribution.

The third tier will be people to help you sell the film the best you can, but will be the newer, smaller agencies that don't have as much of an established reputation.

If you go to my website theguerrillarep.com you can download a free AFM resources pack that has a leads sheet template to help you manage this.

ADVANCE CONTACT

If you've got a completed film, and it's ready more than a month or two before AFM, it will be worth reaching out to the Sales Agent before AFM and seeing if you can place the film before the market. If you can, it will help you see revenue much more quickly.

There's a form letter and a few sample emails in the resources pack available at www.TheGuerrillaRep.com. It can also help you track your due diligence.

If you don't hear anything back within a week or two, it can be helpful to follow up with a phone call. Hollywood isn't always great about email, although that's coming from a guy who lives Silicon Valley. In Silicon Valley, it's assumed if you're picking up the phone and calling something is on fire.

But in Hollywood, calling is the way things get done. Putting in a single call can get an answer as to how much interest a sales agent has, and check if they even had a chance to take a look.

If you called and got no answer after your first email, it might not be a bad idea to send one last email. If you don't get a response by then, assume they're not interested and move on.

If they start to show interest, then it may behoove you to read sections 3 and 4 in their entirety to make sure you have a basic understanding of the structure of a distribution deal, and the various media rights types.

If you're just looking to make a meeting about a film you're packaging, and don't have an existing relationship with the distributor or sales agent, then send an email a month before the market, and follow up a few weeks before, requesting a meeting on the last two days.

The first email should be to simply tell them what projects you're bringing to the market and why you think that they'd be a good fit for them. Especially with the first email, you may only get 10-20% of the emails back. If you get 20%, you're actually doing well. Make sure to mention that you'll be attending AFM this year, and would love to talk to them about the project.

Don't be discouraged if you don't hear back from many of them. These people are very busy, and don't always have time to respond. Also previously mentioned, this business is heavily relationship based. They may be waiting to see if they run across you at AFM before responding.

When you request the meetings, try to make them during the last two or three days of the market, the first part of the market is when the buyers are really out and the sales agents are looking to unload what they already have. Showing a little respect and realizing that these people are always going to sell before buying will put you in good standing with the sales agent. Since this business is really all about relationships, your standing with sales agents matters quite a lot.

If you do get a meeting with a sales agent, it would be very wise to follow-up and confirm that meeting a few days before the market starts. Not only does this increase the likelihood that they'll have it on their schedule, but it shows that you're diligent and professional. Your diligence will look good to the sales agent, and the meeting will likely go more smoothly.

It's much better to follow up a few days before the market starts, simply because of the market itself is very hectic. There's a decent chance your message will be missed due to the chaos.

It's important to keep in mind that there's a line between being diligent and being annoying. Diligence is good; annoyance is bad. It's a little tricky to walk that line, but just keep in mind that these sales agents are very busy, and you should remember that they've got other meetings on their schedule, so don't hassle them.

CHAPTER 9 – DEVELOPING YOUR PERSONAL BRAND

In the words of the host of the #1 indiefilm podcast on iTunes, Alex Ferrari, "If you don't think you need a brand as an indie filmmaker, you're wrong."

There's a piece of conventional wisdom that states women decide if they'll sleep with a man within ten seconds of meeting him. It speaks to the power of first impressions. Within the first ten seconds of someone meeting you, you will have been sized up, and every interaction after the first will be influenced by that very first impression. While getting lucky should never be high on your priorities list at AFM or any other professional convention, most business people have a gut reaction as to whether or not they want to do business with someone within a very short window after meeting a person.

This makes it very clear that appearances and the way you dress are of huge importance in finding people who will do business with you at the AFM. An AFM mentor of mine sums it up very simply, "It's a business conference. You need to look like you're there to do business." That said, it's about far more than just developing a look. It's about developing a personal brand. That means managing every aspect of your image and the interactions you have with everyone you do business with. If you want to achieve success in any industry, your personal brand is very important. This is especially true in the Film Industry.

In Marketing 101 it is taught that a brand is the culmination of every interaction and experience that a person or company has with you. On a personal level, this is your reputation. It's not just how you've interacted with people, but what they've heard of you, how they feel about your work, and how they've interacted with various other clips, interviews, and blogs of yours they've found online.

The biggest thing to keep in mind when establishing your personal brand is managing all of your interactions with potential business partners, clients, and especially potential customers. This means that you've got to maintain a certain level of professionalism any time you do business. You've got to maintain a certain level of decorum, and remember that any business is really about the relationships you cultivate.

When you're building your personal brand, the most important thing is that this brand is still you. Distinctively, unapologetically you. People can always tell when your mask gets too thick, and they don't like it. You can even come across as untrustworthy. Branding doesn't ever mean you should do something that doesn't jive with who you are.

That said, when building your brand it's essential to remember that there are some things best left unsaid. Your reputation matters. Think about how you want people to see you, and emphasize those qualities. While reputation is important, character can be even more so.

What's the difference? Reputation is how people view you. Character is how you truly are. The two are indelibly linked, but if you simply focus on your reputation and not your character, then all you've done is built a mask. If the brand you've built is inauthentic people will eventually realize that. With every passing year, authenticity becomes more and more integral to success in the film industry.

Personal Branding isn't about building a phony you; it's about building the best "you" you can be.

THE POWER OF BRANDING

I don't pretend to be famous. In fact, I'm far from it. But it's become relatively commonplace that my reputation precedes me when I walk into a room of filmmakers, particularly in northern California.

I can walk into a lot of filmmaking events in Northern California and know a good portion of the people there. The more surprising part, is that a good percentage of people I've never met know about me. Be it from the first edition of this book, my blog, my podcast, or one of the many podcasts I've appeared on.

In fact, in the two years since the first edition of this book was published, I've become a minor celebrity at AFM itself. I'm continually surprised how frequently I'm recognized. A lot of that is the fact that I focus very hard on creating quality content but that's not the primary reason it's worked so well. The biggest reason my brand has such value is that I've cultivated strong relationships and I provide a large amount of value to every client I work with, every reader on my site, and every listener to my podcast.

Unlike some other reps, I respond to nearly every query that comes into my inbox. I take the time to share the knowledge I can while ensuring that I'm providing a large amount of value to my clients.

Reciprocity

To better illustrate this point, I'll share with you a few elements of my personal brand. The following is taken from my blog (found at TheGuerrillaRep.com/blog). It's an excerpt from a post about the importance of reciprocity. While it's not entirely about personal branding, it is a bit of advice you may find beneficial, as generalized business advice is big at a market like AFM.

Business, like community, is all about reciprocity. Any functional business relationship has everyone involved helping each other and coming out better than when they went in. I'm happy to promote friends' projects, and support fellow filmmakers in any way I can. If someone invites me to like a page, I generally do. If someone sends me an email, I respond within a business day. If someone invites me to an event on a night I'm free, I generally go. Especially if they've been so kind as to add me to the guest list. Although admittedly this has become more of a rarity since the first edition of this book was published.

Maintaining good reciprocal relationships in any business is vital to success, especially when you're starting out. This is particularly true in the film industry. The old adage "It's not what you know, but who you know" is particularly true in this close-knit community. I cannot emphasize enough the importance of your reputation. If you are known as someone others can count on to be there, this will carry you far.

Always being open to helping others is exhausting, but it pays off in the long run. If you've been helping others wherever possible, when you need a favor there are plenty of people to provide it. If you only take favors then it won't be long before you have no one left to help you.

One way you can practice this at AFM is by connecting the contacts you meet. It's important for building a reputation in the community, and while you may not see direct help from every connection you make, your influence will build over time and you'll end up with a far stronger brand and become more and more able to compete in the very small and competitive sphere that is the American Film Market.

YOUR LOOK

We work in show business. Image and appearances matter. Many people underestimate the importance of fashion in the film industry. Take the red carpet as an example. Everyone is dressed to the nines and the starlets are always asked who they're wearing. We're not hardware salesmen, or industrial piping representatives. We sell entertainment, we sell art, and above all we sell an image.

While the last few markets have been surprisingly casual (as of 2015), I still show up in a three-piece suit with a tie. It makes opening conversations far easier; half the time people open them for me. Although I'm sure it helped that in 2015 I was an exhibitor. That said, the suit or dress you wear isn't the most important thing about your look.

The most important thing is that you be distinctive.

Your look is essentially your logo. People need to be able to remember you by it and it needs to be an extension of you. A good friend and inspiration in writing this book once told me that it doesn't matter what's in your bank account. What matters is how you carry yourself. Thanks for the fantastic advice, Tony.

There are ways to look like a million bucks without spending a million bucks. Most cities have consignment stores with great clothes at a fraction of retail price. Often they'll require tailoring, but in the end that is still far cheaper than buying the suit at a department store. In fact, most times you can find a high-end designer suit at a discount warehouse price. I've bought Armani suits for $200.

If you do go the consignment route, make sure to know your size. If it doesn't fit right be prepared to shell out for tailoring. It's far better to have a cheap suit that fits well than an expensive one that doesn't. The last thing you want people to assume is that you're wearing your grandfather's hand-me-downs.

Anyone can be distinctive in the way they dress, but it's not always a good thing. One guy I know from AFM always wears a sweatshirt, cheap khakis, and a polo. It's certainly distinctive. He spends a lot of time there, but as far as I can tell he doesn't get much business done.

Again, it's a business conference – look like you're there to do business.

While I recommend a full suit for men, and equivalent dress for the ladies, it's important to wear something you feel comfortable in. Whatever your look is, it needs to be you. You may want to try California casual with the suit and no tie, or the silicon valley VC look with jeans, a button down, and a sport coat.

AFM is really hard, especially if you're not a natural extrovert. It's important that you feel like the best version of yourself possible, and the way you dress is a natural extension of that. People will remember the little things about your appearance and little things add up to meaning a whole lot more.

With that in mind, don't forget about hygiene. Comb and style your hair; people will notice. Shave every day before you go to the market. A little bit of facial hair is fine, especially if you're a director or cinematographer, but you should make sure it's trimmed and professional-looking. Brush your teeth. Carry some mints or gum to make sure your breath is always as fresh as possible. Studies have been done that show smell is the sense most linked to memory, and you don't want people to remember you as that guy with bad breath.

A (RATHER LONG) NOTE ON TIE KNOTS (THAT MY EDITOR WANTED ME TO CUT)

Apart from the vest, one of the ways I distinguish myself is with a fancy tie knot. Admittedly, this is a fascination of mine. This is actually thanks to my friend Charles. He recommended this style and I adopted it. There's an old adage that a gentleman knows five knots: the Four in Hand, the Prince Albert, the Half-Windsor, the Windsor, and the Bow-Tie. The Merovingian, the Trinity, and the Eldridge are in a league by themselves. There are dozens of others and it can be a lot of fun learning them.

Adopting these fancy knots has made a difference in how well people remember me, so I share it with you. My personal favorite is the Merovingian Knot. It essentially looks like your tie is wearing a tie. Charles favors the Eldridge. I've done the Trinity, the Double-Eldridge, and a few super-nerdy tie knots as well. These are little things that add up to a whole lot more. And when your brand becomes recognized, that's when you know you've gotten somewhere.

While most people who don't wear a lot of ties generally favor the handover knot (or four in hand) for it's ease, it looks sloppy. While you may not think it matters, people who wear suits regularly will notice, and you never want to look sloppy.

The Windsor is the standard and it's not difficult to learn. When I was learning, I would pull up a video on the Internet and tie along with it. There's a link to a few of my favorites in the resource packet. After a while it becomes second nature, but until it does the guide can be really useful.

I said in the first edition of the book that that I wanted to see more fancy knots at AFM, and boy did people listen. I think part of that is just the fact that fancier tie knots are becoming commonplace across the country, but I'd like to note that I did point it out before it was cool. Some people call that being a tastemaker. Others call it being a hipster. No matter what you call it, patting yourself on the back for it is a bit pompous. So let's get back to useful advice.

Ladies, it's even easier for you to be distinctive in your dress, as business attire for women is much more flexible. You might not wear a tie, so become known as "that woman in the Hermes scarf."

YOUR FASHION BUDGET

Unless you're in finance, you're probably going to have to drop some money on your clothes for AFM. Believe me, I've been in a position where there was very little expendable income to be had. It's worth taking a few extra shifts or sacrificing a few meals out in order to get some good clothes for AFM. Filmmakers who want to achieve success should embrace the following fact: when you're dealing in business, it's important to remember that people will judge you based on your appearance. Don't be afraid of it; embrace it and capitalize on it.

If you're staying in a hotel, take the time to iron all your clothes and hang them the first night you get in. Wrinkles don't suit anyone. I generally see at least a few people walking around with wrinkled suit coats; it's unbecoming and just looks sloppy. Take the time to make sure that's not you.

It's better to have a cheap suit that fits than an expensive one that's way too big – or worse – way too small. Don't borrow a suit from someone who's not your size.

Clothes from different brands are built for different sizes. For instance, if you're a bit more of a short and broad frame, then try shopping at The Gap, Banana Republic, or Versace if you're on the higher income end.

If you're on the skinnier side then H&M, Calvin Klein, Hugo Boss, and

Armani are better brands.

If you're athletic, Tommy Hilfiger is a good fit.

It may be easy to overlook, but shoes are important. There's some psychological evidence that the first thing we check out when sizing up someone is their shoes. Keep it in mind. It's worth spending a little extra to get good ones, even if it means you have to skimp a bit on the suit. You can find some great shoes at DSW in the clearance section. I got mine for 70% off.

A FEW FASHION TIPS

Here are a few quick pointers for people who don't do fashion. I'm passing this advice on from a friend named Lucas Dougherty, who has far more expertise in the subject than I do.

FOR MEN

In terms of suits, a basic charcoal or navy is strongly favored over black or the more fashion-forward colors (lighter suits, earth tones, and the like). Never mix black and brown, black and navy, navy and charcoal, black and charcoal, or grayscale and earth tones. A suit is not a sports jacket; your pants and coat should match.

Keep it simple: a dark suit, a light, unobtrusive shirt, and an interesting tie. If wearing multiple striped or patterned items the spacing on the items should be as diverse as possible; a broad stripe on the tie with a solid shirt and thin stripe on the suit would be an example of this. If you wear a pocket square, it should match a minor color in the shirt, but a perfect match is best avoided.

If you plan to negotiate, power colors are classically used to assert dominance. This can serve as a much-needed leverage piece and you should use every possible advantage. Finally, the belt and shoes of any outfit should be as closely matched as possible. Take your dress shoes with you when you go belt shopping.

FOR WOMEN

Most of this chapter has been focused on fashion for men. AFM has traditionally been a boys club, and it can be more difficult for women to break in. It's a bit of an old-world mentality, so it's wise for women to accentuate their femininity while maintaining a strong professional air. It's worth investing in a few pencil skirts and heels.

Lucas offers these tips for women:

"Accessorize tastefully. If you're wearing a dark suit or sweater, and your shirt is understated – white or pastels – choose a scarf, tie, or bow tie to liven up your outfit. Just remember, less is more; a splash of bold color gets the point across more tastefully than a barrage of 'fashion-forward' choices."

While heels are the classic choice, select sensible but professional footwear based on your personal comfort level. Both heels and flats can be professional in the modern market and remember, you'll be on your feet much of the day.

There are four types of dress for women: Romantic, Classic, Dramatic, and Eclectic. Stay true to yourself while choosing professional clothing that suits you and fits your style. You don't have to dress like a man to be taken seriously.

SECTION 2: AT AFM

CHAPTER 10 – THINGS TO BRING EVERY DAY

While everything I've mentioned so far is necessary, it's important to think about other support items you should bring to the market. Here's of list of these things and a brief description of why you should consider them. For ease of reference, I've included a list of everything you should have on a single page.

1. Business cards
2. Postcards
3. One-page treatments
4. Executive summaries
5. Branded folders
6. Screeners
7. Calendar app/datebook
8. Sales agent and Distributor notes
9. Padfolio
10. Accordion file
11. Receipt file
12. Non-perishable snacks
13. Caffeine
14. Hand sanitizer
15. Self adhering bandages
16. Cash

BUSINESS CARDS

While this topic is thoroughly covered in the printed materials section of this book, the importance of business cards cannot be overstated. If you bring nothing else, bring these.

POSTCARDS

Postcards are useful while pitching, and sales agents prefer this size onesheet for ease of reference. Just remember, these are not allowed in the lobby. If security sees you giving them out it can lead to hassles. You'll primarily use these in meetings with sales agents.

ONE-PAGE TREATMENTS

In case a distributor or sales agents ends up interested in your wares, it's good to have something you can pull out about each of your projects for ease of follow-up. You should be able to pull it out smoothly and hand it to them. If you've made a meeting with a sales agents, it would be wise to put this in a folder along with your other printed materials.

SCREENERS

If your film is completed and you pitch it well, a distributor or sales agent will often request a screener. You'll end up with a far more productive market if you can hand them a hard copy immediately as opposed to sending them an electronic screener later.

Again, make sure your film is copyrighted, and include the registration number on both the disc and promo materials. There are sharks who may be looking to pirate your movie. I don't recommend giving out screeners on the floor, but in offices you're generally pretty safe. It's also considered safe to give it to people with purple or green badges.

This is not a hard and fast rule, and there is always risk involved, but you must share your movies with distributors and sales agents if you're going to make money on them. It's a calculated risk, and copyrighting your film is the best safeguard.

EXECUTIVE SUMMARIES

This is the first section of your business plan. It gives an overview of the project on a single page. If you happen to meet financiers or fund managers at AFM, these will be helpful. Make sure they provide your contact information. This is something that you should only bring out in meetings, but you should have them available with you on the floor in case a meeting comes up without much notice. For advice on writing these please refer to the recommended reading section.

BRANDED FOLDERS

Keep a couple of branded folders with you when you attend AFM. They're important during meetings, and you will likely have more than one meeting on the same day, so have what you need with you so you're prepared for impromptu meetings on top of those you have scheduled. The meetings section lays out everything you should have in your folders.

A CALENDAR APP/DATEBOOK

You may have the opportunity to make an appointment for a meeting in the lobby, on the bus, or while dining, so it's important to write them down so you don't forget.

Generally you'll be told to make an appointment with an assistant once you have access to the office floors, but it's good to be prepared.

DISTRIBUTOR/SALES AGENT NOTES

Have your notes on sales agents printed and accessible, so you can subtly reference them if you happen to meet one of the sales agents you vetted on the floor in the lobby. Make sure you note all meetings next to your research; recognizing the people you bump into can make a huge difference in your reception. It's also productive to look over your notes when you're a little tired of networking and are looking for something useful to do on a break. The more familiar you are with your notes, the more information you'll have at your disposal once you have access to the upper floors for meetings.

PADFOLIO

When you go into a meeting, take notes. Take a professional Padfolio with you. It looks more professional than a notepad and allows you to carry things like a pen, card file, and other necessities with you. It looks professional and organized, which generally bodes well for your personal brand.

ACCORDION FILE

It's important to have a good organizational system that allows you to access your paperwork and printables quickly. An accordion file looks professional and keeps you prepared and organized. As stated, appearances are very important and looking organized, professional, and prepared will carry you far in a professional setting like AFM.

RECEIPT FILE

Everything you spend at AFM is considered a write-off, so keep every receipt you get. The easiest way to keep them organized is with a receipt file. They're generally less than $10 at an office supply store, and they'll save you more than that in time, aggravation, and taxes. It will also make your accountant very happy with you.

Keep it with you, so it's easy to add your receipts as you go. I organize mine in the following fashion:

1. Food and drink
2. Printing and office supplies
3. Travel (cabs, gas, parking, etc)
4. Lodging
5. Miscellaneous

NON-PERISHABLE SNACKS

You're on your feet all day networking, so it can be difficult to keep your spirits up. Keeping your energy high is important, so a granola bar can be a lifesaver at the market. The food at the market is pretty good, but it's a tad expensive. Bringing your own protein bars or similar snacks can save you money.

The food at AFM comes with a convenience and opportunity charge. If you eat at AFM, then you don't have to leave – and you never know who you'll meet while you're in the lobby. By staying in the lobby to network, I once met a Chinese buyer with whom I now have a very good relationship. And the food is tasty, so my advice is to stay at AFM for meals, but bring your own snacks. That is, unless you go get delicious jerked chicken down the street at Cha Cha Chicken.

CAFFEINE

It's not necessary to bring your own caffeine. There's a coffee shop at the back of the lobby, and it's not that much more than getting a regular cup of coffee at Starbucks: generally about $4 for a cup of coffee or $5 for a latte. They also have pretty good croissants. And standing in line in the lobby can be a great place to meet people. One of the most promising sales agents I met was waiting in line to get a latte. He even bought my latte, so that was a double win.

HAND SANITIZER

One of the first markets I went to I ended up coming out of a bathroom stall and seeing a relatively famous person walk by me. I followed him as I walked out of the stalls to the sinks, and he just kept walking. I washed my hands then headed out.

Not 30 seconds after I walked out, a contact hailed me over to talk to him and said, "Ben! Meet [Nameless Celebrity]!" He immediately offered his hand to shake. At this point, I feel a bit like I'm in an episode of Seinfeld and I'm not entirely sure what to do. After a split second, I took his hand and shook it. What could I do?

I ended up going straight back to the bathroom and washing my hands again, and vowed to keep some hand sanitizer on me in the future. Even setting the unusual aside, if you're working the market like you should, you'll shake hands with hundreds of people over the course of the week.

You might end up a little sick after the market. I have after about half of the ones I went to. Communicable diseases fly around like wildfire, given how many people are talking and shaking hands. It's also important to note that paper can carry germs just as easily as hands, so don't just carry hand sanitizer. Use it.

SELF-ADHERING BANDAGES

If you're not used to wearing dress shoes, or you've bought new shoes for the market, they may leave you with blisters. If your shoes are rubbing you red, applying a bandage over the tender spots early can stop that irritation from becoming a blister.

Trust me, you don't want a blister when you'll be on your feet networking all day. It's quite literally a giant pain. This tip has saved my life several times and I generally keep a pack of bandages in my briefcase for just this reason.

CASH

Some places don't take plastic. There are often little incidental costs you'll need to cover with cash whether it's a taxi, the bus, or a tip. An experienced distributor friend of mine recommends bribe money to get things done in a quick fashion. Personally, I've not had to get anything done that quickly attending as a Guerrilla Rep, but it's a good idea to be covered in the case of any eventuality.

THINGS NOT TO BRING

Just like there are many things you might not think to bring, there are some things that you might think you need that are actually unnecessary, might make you look bad, or actually endanger your projects. It's a short list:

1. Scripts
2. Full business plans
3. Laptops

SCRIPTS

There's a pretty big risk of Intellectual Property (IP) theft at AFM, so before you give out any script you must get a signed Non-Disclosure Agreement. Although most of them will just say they don't have much interest in them. A lot of distributors and sales agents focus heavily on completed projects. It's not likely you'll need it.

It's way too easy for a sales agent or distributor to steal a script, and some of them actually will. Also, AFM is super busy so no one will have time to read a script until after the market, anyway. If they request a script, get one of your non-disclosure agreements signed – on the spot, if possible.

FULL BUSINESS PLANS

The same IP theft rules apply here, though to a lesser extent, but it's very unlikely you'll need it. It's not a bad idea to bring a copy or two, just in case, but they're expensive to print and rarely requested. Sales agents and distributors know the potential revenue for your project better than you do, since they have access to confidential information that's very difficult to track down.

Bill Brown, the man who got me going to AFM, shared this piece of wisdom with me. He brought full business plans with him the first time he came to AFM and he ended up not giving many (if any) of them out. You won't need more than two copies, in any case. If you've made the most out of AFM you'll need to substantially rewrite your plan after the market, anyway.

LAPTOPS

When I published the first edition of this book, there really wasn't much of a reason to bring a laptop.   There is more of a reason now. AFM has started allowing a few devices on the wifi, and a lot of laptops are quite light.

That said, your focus should be on networking, not staring in your screen. You may end up using your laptop very little, but unless you have a macbook air or netbook, it probably makes more sense to bring a tablet. You'd be surprised how much an extra 8 pounds can weigh you down over the course of a day.

CHAPTER 11 – MANAGING YOUR MINDSET

So you may be reading this thinking, "Mindset? Why does that matter? I bought this book for practical tips, not existential bologna". If so, think again. This chapter may be the most important one in the book. Success at AFM has everything to do with your mindset and mood.

AFM is about attracting business people and getting business done. In order to do that, you need to know what you're talking about, what you're selling, and have some working knowledge of distribution. More importantly, however, you need to be the type of person people want to do business with. That is all about mindset.

More than likely, all of the sales agents you'll be talking with will know far more about distribution and traditional film monetization than you will. That's how it should be. It takes everything most filmmakers have just to make a film; it's an entirely different skill set to sell one. You need to know enough to not make a fool out of yourself, but all of the people in these offices are experts. They often have decades of experience, so it's a good thing they know more than you.

The most important thing you can do is be genuine, approachable, and likeable. Unless you are primarily a people person that takes a lot of energy, so you need to make sure to manage your mindset while at the market. Here are some tips and advice garnered from my experience at AFM.

IT'S OKAY TO BE OVERWHELMED AT FIRST

In fact, if you're not a little overwhelmed when you first walk in you may not realize exactly how big this place is. AFM is the biggest market for film in the US and just attending puts you miles ahead of many other filmmakers.

There are people here who have had a hand in the biggest productions in Hollywood. There are people here who can get your film seen, so it can make money and you can build a career. That's a lot of pressure if you're not used to high stress business situations. The first time I walked into the lobby at Loews I was petrified.

I've since seen that same petrified look on dozens of filmmakers faces. Whenever I see them, I'll often step up and say hi. Someone did that for me and it helped immensely.

While it's totally okay to be overwhelmed, especially on your first day, it's not wise to show you're overwhelmed. That would open you up to be targeted by some of the sharks patrolling the waters. On your first day go to the market, feel it out, meet a few people, then take a break. If you take the elevator down to the first floor of the Loews hotel, and walk out the back door, you'll find it's less than 100 feet before you hit one of the sandy beaches of Santa Monica.

MARKET HACK #2 – THE BEACH IS RIGHT FREAKING THERE.

If you find yourself overwhelmed, give yourself fifteen minutes to walk and collect yourself. Bring your smartphone, play some music, take off your jacket, and get in a good headspace. I wouldn't stay too long though, because you're in a business suit, not a bathing suit and you'll get funny looks. Sure, it's a bit hot on the beach in a full suit, but it's still nice to take a breath and enjoy the fresh sea air.

Keep in mind you're living most people's dream. You're not selling mutual funds, you're not selling used cars, you're selling entertainment. It's fun, so have some fun while you're selling it. You got into film because you love it, so keep a professional air but have fun with it. It'll make the market go better for you.

MAKE YOUR CAR/HOTEL YOUR SANCTUARY

When I'm going into the market, I generally rock out in my car listening to the music that brings me up and puts me in a good networking and selling mood. Starting the day in a good mood makes staying in a good mood a lot easier, so take the time in your car or however you're getting to market to find that market mindset.

If you're staying in a market hotel, take a few minutes before you leave to psych up. Rock out on your headphones, do your yoga – whatever gets you feeling awesome. There's excellent networking on the busses, so you don't want to be doing your psych up there. Find someplace before the networking opportunities begin to build yourself up and get yourself market ready.

MAKE SOME FRIENDS

Another important part of managing your mindset is making friends. This will be covered more in the next chapter, but AFM is incredibly cliquey. Once you meet some people, go back and talk to them when you need a break, solidifying that friendship. In fact, once you've been going for a few years, it kind of becomes like a High School Reunion. You get to see everybody you haven't seen in a year, find out what they're up to, what they're pitching, and everything new in their lives.

This becomes even more true once you start going to other markets, and it's part of the reason why this business is so heavily relationship based. The exhibitors maintain their relationships with buyers at markets like AFM.

Some people I consider to be close friends are people I met at the market. I stay in touch with them now and some will even put me up when I have to make that occasional trip down to LA. Don't underestimate the people you meet at AFM and keep in mind that you can make friends as well as business associates there.

MARKET HACK #3 – BODY LANGUAGE TRICKS

Now I really sound like I'm talking mumbo jumbo, but these seriously work. Most of these are things I learned from watching too many TedTalks and other internet articles that scroll across my social feeds. A few of these you'll have heard before, but not taken too seriously. Take them seriously and give them a try before you write it off as nonsense. A lot of this is based on the mind-body connection and since we all know how to consciously control our bodies, doing so can really help to adjust our mindset.

1. Smile

Practice smiling. Always have a smile on your face at the market, even if you're tired. I know it sounds hokey, but it seriously changes the way you think and makes it easier to stay happy. Just like your mother always told you, it really does help to turn that frown upside down. It makes you more approachable and since this is all a people game, approachability is vital to your success.

2. Alpha Pose

Keep yourself in Alpha Poses while you're waiting. An Alpha Pose is a strong, dominant stance; the Superman pose is a prime example. This will help you be more assertive in the way you think and act, and can actually help you attract people to talk to. Remember your mother's advice and stand up straight. If this is not your habit it may be hard to get into at first, but once you get used to it, it becomes second nature very quickly. Again, this has a lot to do with the mind-body connection.

That said, you don't want to walk around with your hands above your head or looking like Superman. You may need to take a moment and go to the bathroom and stand in the stall for a few minutes. I've seen a sales agent or two do it while using the urinal and striking up a conversation.

There's some of this in Tai Chi; it has to do with lining up the Chakras so your energy flows better. From whatever source you get it, standing openly and making yourself big will adjust your mindset and help you think and act more assertively. You will also look more confident and people are attracted to confidence.

And as I'm sure we're all well aware, good people are nothing if not confident.

3. Breathe Deeply

Whenever you're going into a meeting or have a moment to yourself, take a second to collect yourself. Pause and take a deep breath, then go back at it full force. This is particularly important before office meetings. Take a deep breath and focus. Collect your thoughts and center yourself. It takes less than 30 seconds, but it makes all the difference when you're getting ready to talk to people.

Taking a deep breath before a meeting can not only help you to center yourself and collect your thoughts, but will also help you appear cool, calm and collected before you enter a meeting. Centering yourself like that also has some other really cool benefits that we'll go over in the exhibitor meetings section.

CHAPTER 12 – THE LOBBY

So you may be thinking, "Why on earth would I want to go to a hotel and hang out in the lobby for half a week?" To start, it's a trick that's used by many conventioneers across industries.   In fact, most of the success I had in the early part of my career came as a direct result of spending time networking in the lobby. The first distribution deal I ever got came from meeting a company's representative through a mutual contact in the lobby.

Hanging out in the lobby for the first part of the market will exponentially increase your success during the latter part of the market. It really is worth the time and expense to spend the first part of the week at the market, even though you won't be allowed to go upstairs. You'd be surprised who you meet talking to people in the lobby, and how it will impact the rest of your market.

It should be noted that AFM 2014 (the AFM after the first edition of this book was published) saw the close of the pool area to non-badge holders. However, this strategy is only mildly less effective.   The lobby may get more crowded a few days into the market, but the extra crowding makes it easier to open with people. If you do get the full market badge, it's easier to open by the pool. You just ask if a seat is taken, play on your phone for a bit, then strike up a conversation.

Your biggest goal in the lobby is to meet as many people as you can. You never know who will pay off and introduce you to the person you need to know. There's food in the lobby that is pretty tasty, albeit a little overpriced.

If you can afford it, eat in the lobby. If not, you can take lunch at Cha Cha Chicken down the street. This is a pretty common tactic for seasoned AFM-ers and I've actually met some pretty powerful people waiting in line at Cha Cha, including the head of a very large entertainment banking division.

Following are some tips on how to find success working the lobby at AFM.

REGARDING FILMMAKERS

It's great to know as many filmmakers as you can; they can really help in getting your projects completed once you have distribution and financing in place. If you've already got a completed film, then they might be able to help you with your future projects. You can meet some great contacts that you can develop projects with, get script feedback, and generally work together with to break into the industry.

However, if you're a filmmaker, you're not going to AFM to meet other filmmakers. You're going there to meet sales agents, attorneys, and maybe an occasional buyer. It should be noted that there are a lot of buyers who just won't want to talk to you. They want to do business with established entities and generally choose to do business only with sales agents who have been around a while.

Towards the end of the market, when you can pick up attendee badges, AFM becomes a bit overpopulated with filmmakers with projects to sell. While there are definitely some of those people at the beginning of the market (hopefully you'll be one of them this year), there are far fewer than at the end.

Buyers often see everything they need to see during the first few days of the market and are tired and less open to talking to people towards the end. Hands down, the best time to meet and talk to buyers is at the beginning of the market. Although, the people you want to talk to are sales agents.

That said, when you do meet fellow filmmakers take the time to talk to them. Ask about their projects and genuinely listen to them. If you have met someone who could help them, provide an introduction. You never know who might return the favor. This is how I got my first distribution deal. A friend introduced me to one of their friends, we got a meeting, and made a deal.

In the past, I've had filmmakers who viewed talking to me as a waste of time, because I had a lowly red badge. They were continually badge-checking other people to see if they could get into conversation with an exhibitor or a buyer.

This woman did see a buyer passing by. She abruptly left the conversation we were having. She approached far too strongly and while they were polite and took her DVD, I saw it on a planter a few minutes later.

FOR EXTROVERTS

If you're an extrovert, it's pretty easy to walk up and open a conversation with people you don't know. You already do this naturally; walk around and when you catch someone's eye, say hello. Introduce yourself and then ask the other person what they're selling.

You're more likely to make a good connection if you ask them about themselves first. If they beat you to the punch, answer politely and then ask them about their wares in return, and listen with genuine interest. Then remember what they have, so you can help facilitate introductions where possible. These same people may introduce you to someone you need to know down the road. That's the way the networking game works and you must play it if you want to find success at AFM or any similar environment.

Remember, people have a tendency to be a little narcissistic and love to talk about themselves. You're far more likely to make a contact at the market if you devote time to taking a genuine interest in people. The film industry thrives on social currency, so knowing and making friends with people can take you far. If you're fun to work with and a joy to be around, people are more likely to want to work with you. Distributors and sales agents are people too, so treat them like it.

FOR INTROVERTS

The lobby is full of people getting business done, running between meetings, and waiting for their next meetings to start. There's a lot of mingling and networking. If you go to the back of the main lobby, there's a coffee shop and a bar on the right just before you head out to the pool. All these lines are places to talk to those around you. The pool area is also a great place to meet people and offers more seating than the lobby area, assuming you have a badge to allow you entry.

There are a few booth-like areas where you can sit and have a conversation. Generally, this seating is at a pretty high premium. There are far more people who need seats than there are seats available, especially with the pool area closed unless you have a badge.

If you're an introvert, you can use the tactic of finding a good place to sit, then camping and waiting for people to come sit with you. People will come and go as they run between networking and meeting other people, so you'll be able to meet people as they run in and out of the booth. It's easier to strike up a conversation with them if you're both already sitting. It's a little hard to meet buyers this way, but it's always hard to meet buyers without an office, so it's definitely still a workable strategy.

I've found this to be less effective than walking the floor and finding people to talk to. Don't go sit in a corner by yourself and expect the people you need to meet to flock over to you. If you are choosing the "camp and wait" tactic, choose your seat carefully to be in the thick of the action. You can also mix these tactics while you recoup energy from walking around and talking to people.

Camping in a booth can work for sales agents, but it's not always easy. By far, the best way to meet sales agents is walking the upper and lower floors in the latter part of the market.

THE AFM PACK MENTALITY

AFM is very cliquey. People tend to gather in groups and say hello to people they know. When you're first starting, it can be difficult to talk to anyone. As your network expands, it becomes easier and easier. Once you've got your AFM clique, they will introduce you to people and you will get more business done.

The hardest part about going to AFM the first time is meeting the first people you'll have to talk to. If you're unknown, nobody really wants to talk to you, but once you become a face at the market, opening becomes far easier. The way you're dressed also plays a significant role in how easy it is to get a conversation started.

A friend of mine once met a very prominent screenwriter (he wrote a few comic book movies you'll have heard of) at AFM. This same friend is the person who taught me the camping strategy. As an introvert, he was having trouble opening with this successful screenwriter. He ran into the screenwriter at the market a year or so later.

The screenwriter felt sure he knew my friend, but he couldn't place where they'd met. The screenwriter asked my friend if he was at this party or that party, or this event. He went on and on about the places they may have met, and eventually my friend said in exasperation, "Oh yeah, that was it."

My friend did not know the screenwriter from that party at Bojack's Place. The screenwriter knew my friend from seeing his face at AFM and my friend made a powerful contact just because he always went to the market. Once the screenwriter and my friend were became friends, he told the screenwriter what happened and they shared a laugh.

But a word of warning: Like in high school, you have to be mindful of who you hang around with. The people you spend time talking to are the people who will likely be associated with you. You don't want to fall in with a bad crowd. This is because to some level, people will associate you with the crowd you associate with. So if you get in with the right crowd, some pretty awesome opportunities can open up for you.

You may be asking, "Are there bad crowds at AFM?" Unfortunately, the answer is, "Yes". There are sharks, some pirates, and other people who just won't help you grow your filmmaking career. Just like in any sort of community, there are those who are going to be more successful than others. Some people just have a vibe about them that you really don't want to get involved with, and unfortunately there are some of these groups at AFM. There aren't too many, but they are there.

I wouldn't spend too much time worrying about the cliquey nature of AFM; I'd just focus on getting as much business done as possible. Try to meet as many exhibitors and buyers as you can. If you can do that, your time at market will be well-spent. Also, by focusing on getting business done, you'll be more likely to end up in the crowd you want to be in.

WHAT TO DO WHEN YOU SEE AN EXHIBITOR

Exhibitors will pass through on their way to somewhere else, so you might run into somebody you recognize from your research. If you do, say hello and that you are looking forward to talking to them later in the week. They may or may not remember you later, but if they do it can break the ice in a powerful way and make your meeting go smoother.

Don't interrupt them if they're clearly trying to get somewhere. Remember your manners. You wouldn't like it if someone stopped you while you were rapidly trying to make it somewhere; odds are they won't like it either.

So this story didn't happen in the lobby, but it proves this point very well.

It was the first day of the market, and already going on about 7PM. I hadn't gotten as much done as I would have liked, because the market was off to a bit of a slow start. So I went to an English pub in Santa Monica called Ye Old Kings Head for some shepherd's pie and a pint.

When I got there, I saw an exhibitor had rented out the other side. It happened to be one I knew, so I checked if I was on the guest list. Sadly I was not, so I went to get my shepherd's pie.

While I was sitting there, I noticed the two Korean gentleman next to me had badges on. They turned out to be buyers. I handed them some promotional materials. There was a lot of interest and we scheduled a follow-up meeting. I finished my shepherd's pie and double IPA then stepped outside.

I realized I wanted a cigarette (doesn't happen often, but it does happen occasionally), so I bummed one from the Santa Monica gutter punks bumming around outside. Now I should note, these were Santa Monica gutter punks, which are a bit different from the West Oakland variety. They were asking about what was going on and why all those people had badges on. I briefly explained what AFM was and they skateboarded away.

I leaned against the light pole and took a drag of my cigarette. I then noticed a beautiful young woman with a green badge standing outside the party I wasn't invited to. So, I walked over and asked how her market was.

"Honestly, it's a bit overwhelming." she said.

"On the first day?" I asked.

"It's my first market" she said. "and I think it's a bit different for you than it is for someone like me. I mean, everyone else is here selling and I'm here buying."

I replied, "I totally understand."

"You do?" she asked.

"Yes" I responded. "Generally, I equate the way a buyer is viewed at a market like this to how an investor is viewed at an entrepreneur

114

networking event in Silicon Valley".

"And how's that?" she asked.

"Well, in Silicon Valley an investor at an entrepreneur networking event is like one of five women in a crowded singles bar. Sure, you're going to get a few offers, you might eve get one or two you really like. The only thing that's certainly going to happen is you're going to get a bunch of assholes who won't leave you alone".

"Yes!" she said, then added, "What are you here selling?"

We closed a not-small deal in after-market follow-up.

The moral of the story is: don't be that jerk who won't leave the exhibitor or buyer alone.

THE PROS AND CONS OF SHOWING UP EARLY

The market is pretty dead before 10AM, but there are a few people around starting at 9AM. Depending on your ability to stay late and your stamina for staying active and alert during the day, it really can be to your advantage to show up early.

Showing up early allows you to settle into the market and generally get comfortable before the crowd arrives. The biggest advantage is the fact that most of the people who do show up right at 9AM are exhibitors and buyers – the very people you hope to meet. Early risers tend to associate well with other early risers.

I've met some really powerful people who run film funds and more than a few buyers by showing up right at 9AM. The big problem is finding an opening. Most of the time they're absorbed in the trade papers available at no cost at the entrance and it can be hard to strike up a conversation. That said, if you can find an opening you can meet some powerful people. You never want to be rude. Better they don't remember you than they remember you as "that guy", so go early and use good judgment.

Remember, while you may want to talk to buyers, they may not want to talk to you. Many buyers will only deal with sales agents and exhibitors, so you may be better off focusing your energy on finding and getting into parties at AFM.

The other consideration is how much going early will affect your ability to stay late. There's a lot of opportunity between 5PM and 8PM and the liquor is flowing when it starts to get late. You may even get invited to a party. AFM does take place in Santa Monica, which is part of the greater Los Angeles area. We've all heard stories of LA Traffic and they're particularly true at rush hour.

THE CLOSING RUSH

The lobby can be a little slow during the day, but it's important to save energy and stay after 5PM. At 5PM, the offices close up shop and everyone comes down to the lobby for a drink. That's the best time to meet sales agents and exhibitors at AFM.

Most of them are tired and a bit overstressed from their long day but they're pretty willing to talk to anyone once they get a drink in them. Talking and conversing with them at night can often turn into a meeting later, when you can go upstairs.

Daisy Hamilton (interview transcript in part 4) said she doesn't mind if filmmakers come up and talk to her while she's having a drink in the lobby, but she's done working, so don't try to conduct business. If you're social, show genuine interest, and actually try to make friends, then you can make some powerful contacts and meetings later in the market.

It's better to focus on building a relationship with whomever you're talking to, with limited business talk. If it shifts towards business, ask if you can schedule a meeting for later in the market.

OPENING

Keep your manners in mind. Don't randomly walk up to people in the middle of a conversation; wait for an opening. An opening can be as simple as making eye contact. If you make eye contact with someone, feel free to go over and say hello. The networking game is easier to play than you might think, because everyone is already there to network and everybody needs each other to get business done. Remember, you are not the only one there to play this game.

Never, under any circumstances, walk up to someone and start pitching. Start a conversation first. Ask about their market. Ask what they are looking for. Think of it like talking to a member of your preferred gender in a bar. You never want to launch straight into asking them to go home together, or even their number. First, you break the ice, get to know each other a little bit, and then you start to talk about going somewhere a little quieter.

Be ready to pitch at the drop of a hat. If you start out pitching without first talking, its unlikely you'll find success. In fact, some distributors simply won't work with you if you brazenly walk up and start pitching. I'm sure many people would give you a fake number if you tried that in a crowded singles bar.

MARKET HACK #4 – MIRRORING OTHERS' BODY LANGUAGE

Most of how we communicate is entirely non-verbal. It's not so much what you say but how you say it. When you're meeting people, keeping their body language in mind can really do wonders to the success you have at the market.

One simple trick to really connecting with someone is to mirror his or her body language. Don't do exactly what they do, as that's a bit obvious. Instead, follow what they do and make minor modifications, most likely they won't notice on a conscious level.

Doing this sends a subconscious signal to them that you two are on the same wavelength and it promotes trust. Surprisingly, by doing this well you will end up on the same wavelength as them. With this, the communication becomes easier and you can really build a good relationship with that sales agent beginning with this technique.

One of the biggest things to keep in mind is that calling attention to it will break the magic. Using it badly will do far more to hurt you than help you. There's a good chance that a lot of these sales agents already know this trick. So if you do it they might pick up on it. It's a common sales tactic. It's not necessarily a bad thing if they pick up on you doing it. Game recognizes game and there's often an unspoken respect from it.

Just as with any skill, it takes a while to perfect. I got good at it partly by going to AFM, but also by watching people interact in bars. It's a good idea to practice such interactions. If you live somewhere where networking events are few and far between, a lot of these social interactions can be honed in bars and clubs.

CHAPTER 13 – WHEN YOU PICK UP YOUR BADGE

So now you've been working the lobby for three or four days, depending on which badge you've gotten. The day has finally come for you to pick up your badge and head upstairs to start meeting with sales agents and exhibitors. Here's how you go about it.

SHOW UP EARLY

First, Show up right at 9AM. The market won't be very active before 10:30 or 11AM, but the exhibitors – or at least their assistants – will be there. You can grab your badge, grab some coffee, grab your research and then go around to the offices you've decided you want to talk to.

Go first thing, as soon as your badge kicks in and start making meetings. That is of course, assuming you didn't set them in advance. You will find it much easier to get an appointment if you go early. If you wait too long your time at market will be filled with missed opportunities. Some of the offices you go to might not be open yet, so move on to the next one then circle back after you've made your rounds. If the exhibitor still isn't there when you've made your rounds, head back to the lobby and network.

As mentioned in the previous chapter, it's generally just big wigs that are around early in the morning, so your chances of meeting them are greater than at any other time. Also, picking up your badge right at 9AM will help you avoid long lines for badge pick-up later in the morning.

SCHEDULING YOUR MEETINGS

Directly before you go to schedule your meetings, look at your research. Take a deep breath, and memorize the Three following things.

1. The names of their acquisitions executive and CEO

2. What title you want to talk to them about and why

3. The pitch on the project you want to talk to that exhibitor about

That's all the information you need in your head. If you overcrowd it, then you can be flustered and you won't pitch as well. Put a smile on your face and go talk to the assistant.

When you see their assistants, merely ask to make an appointment with the head of acquisitions by name. Generally they'll ask what you'd like to talk to them about. Tell them you've got a project similar to whichever project on their slate is most like yours. Generally they'll also ask what stage of production you are in. Usually that's all you have to do to get your meeting.

POSSIBLE PROBLEMS

Sometimes, the person you researched won't be at the market, or won't be in that day. In that case, ask to talk to someone else in acquisitions. Generally, the assistant will connect you with the right person.

Sometimes, they'll say the sales agency is not acquiring at the market. If they say that, politely ask if there's someone you can follow up with after the market. If there is, get their card or make note. We'll cover follow-up in the Post-AFM section.

The best reason a sales agent can give for not buying during the AFM I first heard from a friend and former speaker who said, "While we're at the market, we're only selling. You'll be happy that's our policy if we take you on as a client".

Whether they acquire at the market varies a bit from sales agent to sales agent but more often than not, if they are acquiring, it's not until the end of the market, often on the last two or three days, as previously stated.

ALWAYS LET BUYERS IN FIRST

The primary reason these sales agents are there is to sell. If you're ever in a line to talk to someone and a buyer (green badge) goes in front of you, move aside for him or her. Even if they arrive after you, cheerfully let them go ahead of you. It will make a difference in how you're perceived and can get you – if not a better deal – at least a better reputation. I've had meetings go much better because I acknowledged that buyers take precedence over sellers.

USE YOUR RESEARCH

If you can figure out which sales agents you want to talk to based on what they look for in a market, then make sure you do. If your film fits their brand, make sure you emphasize that's why you wanted to talk to them.

I once got a meeting with the CEO of a distribution company because I was able to quote exactly what they said they are looking for on their website. They said they look for low-budget, niche market films with a strong and loyal demographic they can target. I approached the assistant, parroted what they said on the website, and got a meeting straight away.

We didn't end up doing business because our project was too niche market (a comedy of errors about a transgendered woman coming to terms with her sexuality – would be great in '16, not so much in '11).

However, that sales agent told me even though my company didn't have a name yet, he believed we could make it, so we should talk to him about future projects. I still stay in touch with him, and when the right project comes along, we may do business. In fact, that sales agent contributed to Section 4.

ALWAYS BE PREPARED FOR AN IMMEDIATE MEETING

Occasionally, you'll run into the person you wanted to talk to and you'll get taken into a meeting immediately. So make sure you're prepared for it, and be ready to bust straight into meeting mindset.

Ideally, you should schedule one appointment an hour every hour for your last three or four days at the market. This is difficult; I've personally not been able to get more than fifteen or sixteen meetings, but I continue to have that as my goal. However many meetings you get your first year, you will have plenty to do in following up with them after the market. And each year you will find it that much easier to get the meetings you want. My record for screener requests in a market so far is fifty-five. Email me if you beat it with a red badge.

CHAPTER 14 – THE EXHIBITOR MEETINGS

Sun Tzu said in The Art of War, "If you know the enemy and know yourself, you need not fear the result of a hundred battles. If you know yourself but not the enemy, for every victory gained you will also suffer a defeat. If you know neither the enemy nor yourself, you will succumb in every battle".

This book is more a practical guide to working the often-unfamiliar territory of markets like AFM than an examination of exactly how to negotiate a distribution deal. There are people far more qualified than I to write a book on that subject matter. That said, to find success, you really need to keep in mind exactly where you stand in the eyes of most sales agents. In the second edition, I've included a few chapters in Section 3 that can give you a better idea of what to look for.

While no one really knows how many films are made in a year, the best guess I've heard is somewhere between ten thousand and twenty thousand. Only about five hundred of them find any real theatrical distribution. Numbers regarding VOD, DVD, and home video are rapidly evolving and subject to change months after the printing of this edition. But there is quite obviously a huge gap in the number of films made versus the number of films distributed.

Sales agents have far more options for movies they want to distribute than filmmakers have options on sales agents. Quality is key in determining which films get distributed, but it's far from the only factor. Speaking frankly as someone who receives a lot screeners for representation, a lot of movies just aren't that good. In her interview (chapter 18), Daisy Hamilton says the films she seeks out are often much better than the films that are sent to her.

If you have a film that is good, sales agents may well be interested in picking it up. However you need to know you are the person with less negotiating power. It's a very unbalanced equation and if you start thinking you're the greatest thing since sliced bread and your film is the best thing ever made, chances are that you'll only annoy sales agents and won't get any distribution for your masterpiece. But, while you may not have much leverage, especially if it's your first project, you do have a product. Sales agents and distributors need products to sell to stay in business.

A good sales agent-filmmaker relationship is one where everyone wins, and everyone makes some money. Sales agents and distributors need to turn around a lot of product to stay afloat, so they are always looking for new films. However, keep in mind that there are a lot of filmmakers who can supply them with that product. After all, even just a few short years ago filmmaking was the number one major in the US.

You must know your position, know their position, and keep it in mind when you go into the meeting. Now, onto some practical advice on making the most of the meetings you've scheduled.

PREPARING FOR YOUR MEETING

The outcome you hope for from these meetings is to get to know the sales agent and meet them face-to-face. As much as the industry is evolving, as the world becomes increasingly web based, there's still something about having met in person and talked over a deal.

I used to think this was a huge difference between the way film companies operate from the way tech companies operate. But having co-founded a tech company since the first edition, I can say it's not. Many end up better after meeting face-to-face. Jim, my co-founder at ProductionNext and I still meet in person almost every week because we get through a lot more when we do.

All industries rely on face-to-face communication and phone calls, but the film industry relies on them far more than other industries. This is one big reason markets like AFM are still going strong. People in the film industry still prefer direct communication as opposed to email. Especially in the film industry, a working relationship will be far stronger if you've met someone. It's why these people attend these high-priced markets in these high-priced offices.

PREPPING FOLDERS

Since the first edition, I've become less convinced of the value of folders. The most important thing you can do is build a relationship with the distributor/sales agent. If your film is completed, you maybe better off getting your EPK printed in a way that could serve as a DVD case.

However, I believe there's still value in this as an exhibitor talking to buyers, so I'm including this in here.

About half an hour before your meeting, prep a folder with what you're going to need for the meeting. Figure out which of the projects you're pitching. Build your folder so you have everything they may need at the ready. Put the following in a folder.

On the right:

1. Postcard with onesheet
2. Executive summary
3. Marketing plan

On the left:

1. Business card
2. Screener
3. One page treatment
4. Full slate page

This is how I organize my folders. The postcard goes in the front of the right pocket, the executive summary behind it – with a onesheet cover page as the first page of the executive summary, and the marketing plan, topsheet, and revenue projections behind on the right.

On the left the screener is first. Then the treatment, then the full slate page. Get folders with little slits for business cards in them and put your card in that slit. These are called presentation folders and you can find them at most office supply stores.

This layout is based on the sales folder layout I used when working for insurance and financial services.

GETTING IN THE MEETING MINDSET

It might not be a bad idea to go into the bathroom and alpha pose for a few minutes right before the meeting. As mentioned in a previous chapter, alpha posing can realign your brain to make you more assertive and confident.

Be careful not to come across as egotistical. Confidence is great, it's attractive, and it will help you. Arrogance will scare away any hope you have of doing business with people. Of course, if you've been practicing alpha posing, you can make it work in a not-so-obvious way.

Generally, the biggest key to alpha posing is taking up space. Don't curl up into a ball, don't hunch over, stand up straight. Be noticed. It helps. The mind-body connection is very strong and using it will allow you to go in with a better mindset, which will lead to more success.

When you walk into your meeting, make sure you're smiling. Again, mind-body connection. As mentioned previously, smiling does make you happier. People like to do business with happy people who are fun to be around, so being happy going into your meeting will make it more likely that the meeting will be productive.

Right before you go into a meeting, take a breath and collect yourself. Figure out exactly where you are emotionally. Are you happy? Are you confident? How do you feel exactly? Make a mental note of it. I know this sounds odd, but it really will help you in the meeting. Right now you're thinking, "How on earth would this help me?" It's time for another little psychological trick.

MARKET HACK #5 – TAP INTO YOUR EMPATHY

This may sound like a whole load of new-wave mumbo jumbo, but human beings are very empathetic creatures. We tend to pick up on how others are feeling subconsciously. If you know exactly how you feel when you go into a meeting, then when you sit across from the sales agent you're having a meeting with you can actually get a vibe on how they're feeling. It's a trick psychologists, therapists, and counselors use all the time. If you know exactly how you feel and your mood changes when you sit across from the exhibitor, more than likely you're subconsciously picking up on their mood

Subtly mirroring them is another good way to pick up on their mood. If you mirror them, then you'll also find it easier to pick up on their mood and gauge the conversation. It's much better and easier to do this when you're listening rather than talking. This is something you can really only implement with practice. Again, doing this in a bar or club will help you practice it if you can't practice it through networking before you are at the market.

BEFORE YOUR MEETING, MEMORIZE THE FOLLOWING THINGS.

1. **Who are you meeting with?**

2. **What projects are you talking about?**

3. **Why did you want to talk to them?**

4. **What similar projects have they done?**

HOW THE MEETINGS GENERALLY PLAY OUT

AFM meetings are pretty simple. While there's no format you can follow that will work for every meeting, there are some simple guidelines you can use to increase your chances of success overall. Start by introducing yourself with a few pleasantries and friendly banter. Ask how their market is going. Their answer will help you determine whether they want to chat or jump straight into business. Come across as friendly and approachable, but not overly so. Some sales agents will want to get straight to the point, while others will want to chat first. Follow their lead.

One of the biggest keys to developing a relationship with a sales agent is establishing a good rapport and finding someone with whom you can have a good working relationship. In the end, the most important thing in any relationship is trust.

Let them set the tone of the meeting, then follow their lead. Checking your mindset can really help you figure out whether the person you're meeting is more of the straight-to-business type, or more of the talk-a-little-first type.

When the business talk comes around, start by telling them why you wanted to meet them in particular about your project. Call upon the research you did. Mention similar films they have distributed, and any other pertinent information. Then give them the one page or postcard you brought with you and go into your short pitch followed by your thirty-second pitch. At that point, ask if they have any questions.

Generally, the longer the meeting goes, the more likely it is that you'll be able to close something. Many meetings will only last about 5-10 minutes and will result in a lot of after-market follow-up. If you've brought a completed film the meeting will probably be longer. If you brought a screener, there's a chance that they'll schedule a follow-up meeting on the last day so they can watch it.

If you brought a screener and a trailer there's a good chance they'll watch the trailer right there. Make sure it's accessible on your screener without issue. This is why a simpler DVD is better than a DVD with a lot of extra content.

While you can sometimes close deals at the market, it's not the standard. Most of the deals will occur in the after-market follow-up.

Just as there are many shoulds, there are also some should-nots, the most important of which is never lie. If they ask you a question you don't know an answer to, be honest and say you don't know. If it's a weakness with your product, own it. These are business people and dealmakers. They can smell bullshit a mile away. It's far better to not know than to lie. Just say something like, "Good question, I'll find out and get back to you".

That said, you don't want there to be too many questions you cannot answer. There are also some things that you definitely should know. You should know things like what your target market is and a have at least a loose marketing plan for your movie. There are ways of finding out this information, but it's not the focus of this book. To find out more, I'd recommend starting by downloading the free resource packet from www.TheGuerrillaRep.com

In short, it comes back to something I've said before. In this meeting, you may be selling a movie, but what you're really selling is yourself.

CHAPTER 15 – THE PARTIES

Everyone has heard of the yacht parties at Festival Du Cannes and Marché du Film (the worlds biggest and most acclaimed Film Market held in Nice, France). While there are far fewer parties at AFM than there are at Cannes, if you pay attention you could probably find one to attend every night. If you've got the energy for it and are the type of person who can burn the candle at both ends, you can meet some pretty impressive people at parties. A friend of mine danced with Mel Gibson at an AFM party in 2013. You do have to keep in mind that AFM is thoroughly exhausting and sleep can be an important commodity, so use your time wisely.

MY AFM "YACHT" PARTY

During my third AFM, about halfway through the week, someone handed me a flyer that prominently advertised a "Yacht Party". It detailed there would be live music, fine wine, champagne, and available women. I had spent the week working diligently, things were going well, and I didn't see any harm in cutting loose a bit. I invited my assistant and a friend to join us.

We were already dressed up for market, so we networked as much as we could before we headed over to the party. We arrived at the posted address as the party was scheduled to start. It was apparently massive – massive enough to require three packed parking garages to accommodate the cars of the partygoers. My assistant pointed out a few confusing sign postings and none of us could figure out the directions on the flyer.

We made our way down the waterfront, confident in the belief that we could find the place on our own. Shortly into our walk we heard fabulous live music and spotted a few gentleman in tuxedos, so naturally we believed we were headed in the right direction.

Unfortunately, we soon discovered the party was behind a locked gate.

It seemed we had missed the entrance, which was now a mile in the opposite direction. Exchanging glances, we determined we were all fit enough to easily hop the fence. Seeing that the majority of the party attendees were a hundred feet away, we jumped the fence unseen. Suave. Or so we thought.

We made our way inside, found a man in a tux who looked like he might be in the know, and announced ourselves as being from the American Film Market. He grinned and pointed back in the direction from where we had come. "You must be looking for that party."

Our eyes followed his finger. Just off the pier – on the other side of the fence we had just hopped – a small houseboat was docked. We glanced at each other and shrugged. Again we set off, again we hopped the fence – not quite so suave this time, but just as determined.

Finally arriving at the houseboat, we found the "fine wine" they had advertised was actually a very well known brand of wine we fondly refer to as "Two-Buck Chuck". The champagne was the same, from the same well-known market. The "available women" were there as advertised, but they were older divorced women looking for younger men to whom they could attach themselves. The 'live music' consisted of two broke college students with guitars playing "Smoke on the Waters" covers.

I attempted to keep a positive attitude; I grabbed a glass of cheap, bitter wine and mingled with the other guests. It took a while to adjust my expectations, but once I managed that, I had a fairly good time. I met several people, swapped business cards, and went home early. My badge took effect the next morning.

The next day, as I made my usual rounds of the offices, I went to one of the larger offices. I gave my name to the assistant at the front desk, and rattled off the distributor's name I had researched. The assistant fetched the executive, and as he walked out a flicker of recognition crossed my face.

"Ben!" he claps me on the back, "It's so good to see you!" It was a gentleman I had spent time talking to at the "yacht" party. As it turned out, he was one of the more influential producer's reps at the market that year. I should have recognized him the night before, from my pre-market research, but it all worked out happily.

AFM is one of those places where you'll never know exactly who you're talking to at a party or in the town of Santa Monica and its important to remember to not let your expectations or attitude keep you from making an important connection. So have fun, stay positive, and remember, until you are alone in your hotel room you are always "on", always selling yourself, wherever you are.

THE PARTY CULTURE OF AFM

Another thing to keep in mind about AFM parties is that – as illustrated in my story – most are not as hoity-toity as the proverbial Cannes parties. Don't expect them to be, even if they advertise themselves as such. You can still have a lot of fun.

But be careful how much fun you have. I heard a story at AFM about a man who went to one of the parties, got far too inebriated, and picked up a girl and jumped in the pool with her, still in his business suit. While this is the most visual of his transgressions on the night in question, there were other parts of the night that also did not reflect well upon his character.

At the time, this man was a part of AFM's inner circle, and he could get a lot of business done. The next year, he didn't come to AFM. In fact, nobody's seen him at the market since. The only thing that remains of his market experience is this story, which still makes the rounds. Remember, your reputation is important, and how people view you in this business will determine how long and how successful you are in this business.

THROWING A PARTY YOURSELF

Throwing a party at AFM can be a great way to meet people and promote your projects. Generally, it's a tad too expensive for most filmmakers or hot on the scene exhibitors, but if you've got the money it can be an excellent way to get some deals for your film. It's also surprising how cost-effective it can be.

The biggest advantage to the party scene is the ability to generate buzz and get some press. So if you throw a party, make sure it's a blowout.

If you do decide to throw a party, the most important piece of information to remember is to deliver on whatever you advertise. If I had gone into the party expecting cheap booze and a fun little party on a houseboat I would have had a lot more fun from the outset. The best advice I've gotten from a mentor who's thrown some of the best parties in Cannes is this: provide ample food and drinks and make sure your party is a whole lot of fun.

Don't just feed them little nibbles; pretzels and party mix won't cut it. The days at the market are exhausting. Make sure your food is satisfying. Speaking from event planning experience, sandwiches and finger foods are a good way to go. Serve protein and fats with alcohol. Meats and cheese will go faster than veggies and fruit, but you want all three. Hearty is better, as some people will not have had dinner when they arrive.

Don't feel the need to make your entertainment classy, just make it fun. A rock band is probably a better draw than a string quartet. Keep in mind that people have to be able to mingle and talk, so the music can't be overly-loud. It's got to be a fun atmosphere where people can still meet people and do business. AFM is really about business, after all.

CONSERVE YOUR ENERGY

AFM is a lot of work. It's very rewarding, and well worth the time and energy you have to put in to make it a success, but you will be wiped out by the time it's over. I generally go out for dinner with my group of AFM friends – old and new – at the end of market each day. It's a lot of fun and you can really build relationships with your crowd. For me, it also helps to recharge the batteries from the exhausting day. Just remember you're at the market to do business, so save some energy for the next day's work.

SECTION 3: POST-AFM

CHAPTER 16 – YOUR FIRST THREE DAYS AFTER THE MARKET AND WORKING THE HOLIDAY LAG

First, congratulations on making it through your very first AFM – or your second, third, fifth, ninth, or however many you've been to. As stated in the prologue, I was surprised and humbled to hear how many AFM veterans found the first edition of this book useful. Going to AFM is a challenge most filmmakers never set themselves to do. The very fact you've done it is worthy of praise. Unfortunately, the work has only just begun. Most of your deals will take place in the after-market follow up.

The time directly after the market closes is particularly important to long-term success. If you send follow-up emails it's far more likely the contacts you met at the market will remember you. This is key to building a long-term business relationship with them.

That said, you're going to be completely exhausted, and sometimes taking some time for yourself will help you move forward faster than running around in a mania. So on Thursday take some time for yourself. You've earned it. The exhibitors from AFM will be doing the same thing, so it's best to wait and talk to them on Monday, which gives you a good day or two after traveling to recharge your batteries.

UTILIZING CONTACT MANAGEMENT SOFTWARE

When you do get back to work, there are some applications that will help you get the job done faster. I recommend an inexpensive app, available on both iOS and Android, called CamCard. It lets you take a picture of a business card and then enters the information into a digital format you can export via excel or other contact applications. It's great for the producer on a budget. There's a link to it in the resource packet at www.TheGuerrillaRep.com.

It's boring work, since you've got to double-check them all for accuracy, but it's worth doing, as you'll always have your contacts in an easy-to-manage format.

I recommend sorting them the following way, but feel free to customize this to make it work for your business practices:

1. Buyers and distributors
2. Exhibitors and sales agents
3. Financiers
4. Bankers
5. Lawyers
6. Film commissions
7. Other filmmakers
   a. You can also delineate this section by crew positions, cinematographers, directors, soundies, et cetera, which makes it a lot easier when you crew your next project.
8. AFM contacts 20XX
9. AFM 20XX screener requests
10. AFM 20XX individual follow-up
11. AFM 20XX merge follow-up

You can set multiple tags for each card, so setting up an AFM category for all of these is useful. I recommend using as many tags as possible, as it makes searching for contacts far easier when you need to find someone.

You need to follow up individually with at least the first four or five categories. If you have networked as much as you should have, this will take about half a day of emailing, but it's worth doing. The other contacts are better to follow up individually with as well, but you can get away with a merged mass email follow-up if you're short on time and have too many to email individually.

MERGE FOLLOW-UP

Mailchimp is free and easy to use.

You can go to their website and sign up for an account, or check the resource packet for more information. You can send great HTML emails and start a mailing list to keep in contact with all your new contacts.

For the first contact, DO NOT use an HTML email.

Using an HTML email is way too impersonal, and people will be able to tell they didn't get any individual attention. If you use a plain text campaign most people won't be able to tell you sent them a merged follow-up and you can avoid sending forty or fifty individual emails, which saves a lot of time.

It's not bad to do this, because more than likely you would just be copying pasting the information and manually changing the merge tags for this follow-up, so it's just letting the computer do that work for you. I live by the motto: work smarter, not harder. This is one way to do that.

USE MERGE TAGS EFFECTIVELY

There is a setting on Mailchimp to autocorrect any case issues so that it displays properly. It's in the FAQ on Mailchimp and there's an excellent step-by-step guide there that explains this better than I could, here. I highly recommend using it.

WHAT TO INCLUDE IN YOUR FOLLOW-UP

Follow-up is really about staying in your contacts' minds and starting to build a relationship with them. There's an art to relationship management that comes with time, but for the sake of this book and specifically for AFM follow-up, there is a relatively standard process with certain things you should include. Your follow-up email should be pretty basic. Essentially send them an email including the following things:

1. It was nice to meet you

2. I hope your market went well

3. A reminder of who you are, and what you talked about

   a. This is a great place to reinforce your personal brand. For Instance I generally say: I'm Ben, the blonde producer's rep in a three piece suit and fancy tie.

4. A brief, one sentence description of your market and how it went

5. A desire to stay in touch and an offer to help them should they ever need it

6. Optional: ask them if they want to join your newsletter/mailing list, and include a link

   a. If you're doing this, it will be way more effective if you can give them something free for doing so

There are templates to use as an example in the resources packet.

For distributors and sales agents you met at the market, make sure you include all the information they requested. If they requested a screener, make sure you include a Vimeo link even if you sent them A DVD. sales agents get A LOT of screeners after AFM and their workflow can vary, so including a Vimeo screener can help make sure they review your project in a timely fashion.

Remember this business is all about relationships, so structure your follow-up accordingly.

STARTING THE FOLLOW-UP

Most of the deals will come from follow-up, so make sure you do it and do it well. Start your follow-up Monday morning. Contact the people you had meetings with first, then the buyers and distributors, then the sales agents and exhibitors, then the others. The buyers and distributors aren't likely to get back to you, but the sales agents may very well.

About 25-50% will respond to you. That's actually on the higher end of a response rate, so don't feel bad if only 10-25% respond to your email. Should anyone respond to you, make sure to respond within one business day.

As a producer, your contacts are what keep you in business. Going to

AFM is a great way to get more contacts, so make sure to stay in touch with them. Respond to them and help them out wherever possible. Send them an HTML Christmas card to keep you on their minds.

NEWSLETTERS AND MAILING LISTS

If you want to develop an audience and a community, it may behoove you to include an offer to join your mailing list in the filmmaker and merged follow-up. This could help you develop a quarterly newsletter on developments with your projects. If you want to do this, don't simply add people to your email list. Include a link and ask if they'd like to join it. Sure, not a huge amount of people will, but the ones that do will be far more likely to be interested.

Remember, email marketing is all about providing value. Don't email your list if you have nothing to say. Only email them if there's something they would be genuinely interested in. Did you write a fantastic blog? Get into a new festival? Start airing on Netflix? Those are great reasons to blast your list.

Unless you have some fantastic content to share, I wouldn't email your list more than quarterly. You don't want to get blocked for spamming too many people.

THE HOLIDAY LAG

AFM is at a little bit of an awkward time of year. It's only two or three weeks before Thanksgiving and then there's only another week or two before everybody is taking time off for the winter holiday season. If they forget about you during the after-market follow-up, re-establishing a relationship can be hard.

Of course, you don't want a sales agent to ignore you because you're being annoying, either. Deals are being closed at the market far less then they used to be, so sales agents are also closing deals after the market.

Like any good business, they have to get old product out before they get new product in, so letting them sell their current catalog will make them more able to sell your catalog.

CHRISTMAS TREES MAY BE EVERGREENS, BUT FILMS ARE NOT

All films have a shelf life and waiting too long to close really impacts the window of when the film can see a return. It also affects the likelihood of a sales agent or distributor acquiring your film. The first window of a film's distribution only lasts about a year or two. After that point, the potential monetization of the project is drastically decreased. Waiting too long to get your film out there will have a very negative impact on your film's revenue.

That said, make sure not to rush the process and that any deal you take is a solid deal with a solid company. You'll find out more about what those deals look like in the next few chapters.

The biggest keys to successfully working the holiday lag are to follow up the Monday after AFM, and then follow-up regularly enough to not be forgotten, but not enough to be a nuisance.

Given when AFM takes place, and the fact that the sales agents have to first close their deals, closing before the end of the year can prove difficult. That's not the end of the world; I've often closed deals in early-to-mid-January.

You should definitely try to close the deal by mid-January, though. The next market after AFM is the European Film Market (EFM) and it takes place in February. Sales Agents start sending out their promotional information for EFM around the second or third week of January, so if you're in their slate before then you may start getting money sooner.

Unless your deal came with an advance or a minimum guarantee, it's unlikely you'll see much money for the first few months. It may even take a year or so. So plan for that when you're making your financial plans for the next year.

With luck, you'll start seeing some money by the end of the first quarter after EFM. Don't count on this, as the EFM may just involve your sales agent recouping their own expenses. You should definitely start seeing some money after Cannes, which is in May. It often takes eighteen months or so for your film to recoup 60-80% of its budget. That's assuming your sales agent is doing their job and your film is likely to recoup its budget.

Nothing ever really gets done the last week or two of the year. I wouldn't plan to work much those weeks unless you're really close on a deal and one party needs to close it for tax purposes. Take a couple of weeks off, recuperate, and plan your next movie.

CHAPTER 17 – THE IMPORTANCE OF FOLLOW-UP

The importance of following up after AFM cannot be understated. Once the market is over, the deal-making is only just beginning. Gone are the days when indie filmmakers and sales agents made deals in droves at the market. While deals do happen at the market, it's far more common that deals are done in the weeks following the market.

Most of the deal negotiations happen after market, too. This book is not intended to advise on which deals you should take. This book is to help you through the process of deal-making and follow-up. A few chapters that are new to the second edition can help you understand what a deal looks like and gives some general guidelines for numbers in those deals.

The distributors and sales agents you know are the most valuable tool in your tool belt, aside from financiers, executive producers, and angel investors of course. Finding a good distribution deal is essential to furthering your career as a filmmaker. Developing your audience outside of your current reach is essential for growing your career and your production company. Finding the deals necessary to do that is all about the relationships you foster with the sales agents and distributors you meet at AFM and other markets. So when you're following up with the sales agents and distributors, it's important to keep a couple things in mind.

STAY AT THE FOREFRONT OF THEIR MIND, BUT DON'T BE AN ANNOYANCE

It's a bit of a tricky line to walk, but it can be done. If you bug a sales agent every day they'll decline your project simply because they don't want to talk to you anymore. They're incredibly busy and have a lot of filmmakers they work with. It's important to not waste their time, but It's almost as important to not let them forget about you. So, how often do you talk to them?

Personally, I feel an email every five days is about the most you can ping somebody without being an annoyance. I recommend sending an email Monday afternoon, Friday morning (not Friday afternoon, as it often gets lost in the weekend mail), and the following Wednesday morning.

Even that is at least bordering on too much and is assuming you don't hear back from them before you email again. You can only pull off this frequency if they've already shown some interest in you or your project. Generally emailing is safest for follow-up, as it provides a record of your conversation that is admissible in court should things go sour. There are more admissible ways to communicate, but it's at least something of a paper trail.

That said, the film industry is a bit more personal than the tech industry, so if you've not heard back after an email or two, a call might not go amiss, provided they have shown some interest.

If they don't get back to you after a few attempts, assume they're not interested and circle back when you have another film or something newsworthy about your project.

If you've got a project in development, it's going to be really difficult to keep their attention, so don't be surprised if they tell you to come back when you have more in place. If your project is in development without attachments, it may be too early to reach out to a sales agent or distributor with whom you don't already have a relationship. Keep in mind: a sales agent needs films they can turn around quickly and that's just not the case for most in-development projects.

Speaking from personal experience, it's incredibly rare I do anything with in-development projects and I almost never work on an in-development project when I've not worked with the filmmaker before.

PLEASENTRIES ARE GOOD, BUT BUSINESS IS BETTER.

Pleasantries can ease the transition to business, especially in a phone conversation. A quick mention of the weather, or something of the sort makes it easier to open up the talk about business. If someone likes you, they're more likely to do business with you. A sense of humor never hurts, but keep in mind you don't want to offend people. Remember these are business people, so keep the social niceties short. Time is money, after all.

When following up, remember these people are very busy so your conversation should be primarily about business. When talking business, be succinct, direct, and to the point. It's better to spell out what you need to in six words than twelve, as long as you're not rude. For email, take a moment to reread and edit your response before you send it. Better a clear response a few hours later than a sloppy email sent immediately. There is no vocal inflection in an email and no body language, so write your communication in such a way that the recipient doesn't need to read between the lines.

DO YOUR DUE DILIGENCE

Always check out a distributor or sales agent before signing on with them. There's a lot of smoke that flies around the market and a lot of sales agents don't deliver on their promises.

The world of film distribution is incredibly small. Talk to other people about your sales agent, distributor, or producer's rep before you sign with anyone. If you talk to other sales agents or distributors, then you may not get an entirely unbiased or open response. These people see each other at all the major markets and if word gets around they are bad-mouthing other distributors it can be bad for business.

They are also a rather competitive bunch and they're all competing for a shrinking number of buyers. Take what they have to say with a grain of salt unless you know them well. Generally speaking, it's far better talk to the distributor or sales agent's other clients.

TALK TO FILMMAKERS THE SALES AGENT HAS WORKED WITH IN THE PAST

The most important people you can talk to are filmmakers who have had their films distributed by that sales agent or distributor. You can find them by looking the film up on IMDb, then using IMDbPro to look at the specifics. There is contact information for the production company behind the film available on the film's IMDbPro page. When you contact them, be honest about why you're getting in touch. Say you're considering doing business with their sales agent or distributor and wanted to know what their experience was like. Most times they'll be pretty honest with you and give you the real deal on how it is to work with that person or company.

This generally requires a subscription to IMDbPro, but this is a subscription you will need, and it's worth the cost involved. If you ever plan on attaching talent to your film, this subscription is necessary as it provides contact details for actors' representation.

You may even want to ask the sales agent for references. If they balk and lash out at you asking why you would need that, it's not always a good sign. Although, keep in mind if you do ask them for references, they're going to give you the best possible references they can and it may hide some of their imperfections.

ASK YOUR SALES AGENT QUESTIONS

There are a few questions you should ask your distributor before signing anything. Most entertainment attorneys will already know them, as do producer's representatives. If the answers line up, it's a good sign you can trust the distributor. Here are the questions I ask:

1.   Is the Deal Exclusive?
     a. It probably is, and that's not necessarily a bad thing.

2.   What territories do you regularly sell to?

3.   How long will it take for me to see money back?

4.   What happens if I haven't seen money a year (or two) after I

give you my film?

    a. ALWAYS ask for a performance guarantee in the contract.

5.   What happens if the sales agency goes bankrupt?

This list is by no means complete, but it's a start. Once you've gotten to negotiations you should have legal counsel. If you've followed instructions so far, you'll find attorneys' contact information in your contact file from the market.

ALWAYS DO YOUR NEGOTIATIONS IN WRITING

Whenever you're negotiating a deal memo or contract, do it in writing. There's a certain format for going over a contract that's easy to reference. Again, the purpose of this book is not to advise you on which deals to take, but rather the process of deal-making, so the terms listed here are an example of a properly-formatted response.

This sort of response is only appropriate if a sales agent has sent you a deal memo to look over. If they have, this is the standard way to negotiate those terms. It's easy to understand and straight to the point, once you have the formatting down.

First, reference the page with the clause in the contract you want to negotiate. Next, reference by name the section of the contract the term you want to negotiate falls under, then reference the clause and paragraph that term is in, and finally spell out what you to change the term to. In the end it should look something like this:

1. Page 2, Deal Terms, I, B: Territory US and Canada excluding Fr. Speaking Canada

2. Page 2, Deal Terms, I, C: Prefer three (3) years

3. Page 2, Deal terms I, D: Language, English and Spanish only

This is taken from an email chain from a distribution negotiation for a slate of films I represented. There is no proprietary information contained within this example, but you can clearly see the standard format that allows you to talk about the contract without misunderstanding.

Although now that most distributors and sales agents are becoming more tech-savvy, many will just send you a word document you can use the comments function on.

ONCE YOU START NEGOTIATING A DEAL, SEEK PROFESSIONAL COUNSEL

In an interview my co-host Randy Hall and I conducted on the Film Insight Podcast, Entertainment lawyer Daniel Riviera gave some excellent advice. Distribution is a highly specialized skill that takes decades to master. Filmmakers have another craft that also takes decades to master, and it's rare to find someone with both of these skills. It's vital to seek legal counsel or at least the advice of a producer's rep when negotiating these deals.

If you get to the point that you're negotiating a deal memo or contract, talk with an attorney, or at least a producer's rep. A producer's rep is essentially an agent for producers and I happen to be one. They help navigate the often turbulent and constantly changing waters of distribution and film finance. Some are better than others, so research them before you contact them.

If you need a producer's rep, you can contact me through my website. There's a submissions form that you can fill out at www.TheGuerrillaRep.com/submit. I'm not the only producer's rep you can find, but not all of them deliver on everything they say they can. As with a distributor – do your due diligence. The biggest difference between a producer's rep and a lawyer (apart from membership in the bar association) is that producer's reps often but not always work on commission and lawyers charge an hourly rate. This isn't always the case, but it's the general rule regarding brokering tasks.

Legal advice is of the utmost importance when negotiating a deal. Legal counsel or a producer's rep can point out flaws in a contract you would never have noticed and can structure contracts in ways you would never consider. Both lawyers and producer's reps are also more experienced negotiators than most filmmakers.

A lawyer may be expensive, but not as expensive as neglecting to hire one. Legal advice will often end up netting you more than you spent on it through better deal terms. Don't neglect to put legal fees in the budget for your film.

Even if you have a producer's rep, you'll generally want a lawyer as well, but mixing the services of the two can save you money on negotiations.

IT'S BETTER TO HAVE NO DISTRIBUTION DEAL THAN A BAD ONE

Remember, there are other outlets than AFM to get money from your film. They generally require quite a lot of work to produce revenue, but a bad distribution deal will preclude you making any money. A really bad distribution deal won't just stop you from making money; it can even cost you money.

If you only take one thing away from this book, make it this. Don't sign away your film to someone you don't trust. It's your baby, it's your heart, and it's your soul. Make sure you take good care of it and only entrust it to someone who will treat it well and monetize it properly. Even if you can't make money on it, get it to someone who will get it seen so you can make money on the next one.

The next three chapters are new to the second edition and are a guide to what a distribution deal looks like, as well as a guide to self-distribution.

CHAPTER 18 – THE BASIC STRUCTURE OF A DISTRIBUTION DEAL

A lot of people are afraid of the complexity of deals with sales agencies. They have a reputation as being very dense, and difficult to understand. While there is truth to this, there's also a general layout every filmmaker should understand. Many of the pitfalls for distribution can be avoided by knowing these 7 major deal points and the general ranges that fall within them.

This list is not meant to be complete, but it does cover the most important aspects of the deal. Of course, you should always have a lawyer or a producer's rep look over your contract.

TERM

This is not really all that different from the standard legal definition of the term; it's simply how long the contract will remain in place.

For a feature film, a good term is anywhere between three and seven years. During that time, the sales agent will generally be able to sell the film to third parties (i.e. Buyers) for terms that extend beyond the contract with the filmmaker.

TERRITORY

The territories are where the sales agents have the right to sell your film. These rights can be both exclusive and non-exclusive. If you're licensing the film to a sales agent without the help of a representative or a lawyer, there's a good chance you'll be giving them all rights, or at least the vast majority of your rights.

Generally, territories are broken out by both region and country. For example, Germany would be considered a territory in the Western Europe Region. This can get confusing, in that Latin America is both a territory and a region. The region also contains Mexico, Brazil, and a few others.

LANGUAGES

One must keep in mind that the business of international sales a global one (as the name would imply). As such, it means dealing with both cultural and language barriers. Often, a territorial sale is heavily influenced by language.

MEDIA

Media refers to the different Delivery methods that a sales agent can sell your film by. Different rights would include the following:

1. Theatrical

2. DVD/home video

3. PayTV

4. Cable/NetworkTV

5. VOD (Et Al)

For a more detailed breakdown, see the next chapter.

Generally, a sales agent will sell by any combination of these three types of rights. Most of the time, these rights will be exclusive. However, you should hold back PPVOD/TVOD non-exclusively, at least through certain chapters. It's not in your best interest to hold back all of your PPVOD rights, though. It's very difficult for a producer to properly utilize SVOD rights. Additional, most TV deals require SVOD rights as well.

Exclusivity is necessary, and does help the filmmaker as well. Exclusivity is the only thing that creates value when the thing you're selling can be replicated infinitely. If the supply is infinite, there's no way to have enough demand to increase the value of the content. Exclusivity helps maintain the value of the content.

REVENUE SPLIT AND MG

The revenue split refers to the sales agent takes, as opposed to what the Filmmaker takes.

These splits usually vary between 20% and 35%. Generally, sales agents don't like to negotiate this deal point too much. Although there are other ways to make more money from your film than trying to negotiate the split.

A Minimum Guarantee (MG) would be the payment a filmmaker receives up front. While this does happen, it's somewhat rare. Generally, you'll need recognizable talent in a very well-made film in a hot genre to get an MG.

You can sometimes negotiate a split with a sales agent that's different before and after they've recouped their expenses.

RECOUPABLE EXPENSES

Travelling to film markets gets quite expensive, often costing in the mid five figures to the low-mid six figures. As such, in order to stay in business and not charge filmmakers up front, sales agents often charge recoupable expenses. If there was an MG, this would be part of the recoupable expenses.

Generally, filmmakers won't see a cent until the film has recouped those expenses, however it is sometimes possible to negotiate a split that's different before and after recoupment.

You should ALWAYS cap recoupable expenses. Generally, that cap should be somewhere between $20K and $50K, not including any MG. That number could also be substantially higher if there's a theatrical release involved. For a smaller agency, this number may be as low as five thousand dollars.

EXIT CONDITIONS

This is how you exit the contract should things not go well. There are lots of different provisions for this – far too many for this chapter. Here are a few things you could include.

OPTIONAL REVERSION IF X% OF BUDGET NOT RECOUPED BY 18–24 MONTHS AFTER DEAL SIGNING

This would mean that if you haven't made a certain percentage back by a certain date, then the rights would revert to you. Generally you'd put this number at 30–50% in an all rights deal. It's your film, you deserve to get paid.

OPTIONAL REVERSION IF COMPANY IS WHOLLY ACQUIRED BY A THIRD PARTY, OR GOES BANKRUPT

International sales is a risky game, and often the newer players in it don't last long. Because of this, it's important to make sure that you include this clause.

ARBITRATION

Arbitration generally works by having either one or three arbitrators settle a dispute and help assess whether or not there has been a material breach of contract on the part of either party. By settling the matter out of court it supposedly saves the filmmaker a substantial amount of money. However, there are not insignificant costs associated with arbitration.

The base contract from the IFTA has an arbitration clause already in it. The big issue is not simply having an arbitration clause, but having an arbitration clause that works.

In my opinion, your exit conditions are a better place to focus. Arbitration only comes into play if things have gone wrong. The only way you can define whether things have gone wrong is if there's been a material breach of contract. Defining what is a material breach of contract in the exit conditions is the best way to ensure you can have your rights back if someone doesn't hold up their end.

It should be stated that if an arbitrator does become necessary, it is often too late.

CHAPTER 19 – MAJOR DISTRIBUTION RIGHTS

Distribution deals tend to confuse and confound many filmmakers. While there are a lot of complicated places that revenue can get lost, the essence of distribution deals is quite simple. They're essentially just parsing of different media rights to various territories around the world. However, given the black box that is world film distribution, it's often unclear how these rights get structured.

In the last chapter I shared the general structure of a distribution deal. In this one I'll lay out the different rights that most feature film distribution deals parse.

Generally, these rights are broken up both by territory and by type. Sometimes you'll parse out different rights to different sales agents, but that can get counter-productive quite quickly. Sales agents need to have a decent amount of the globe in order to hold sway with their buyers. Sometimes things can be done to parse that a bit further, but it's more than I can go over in this book. The best advice I can give you on that front is to hire a good producer's rep if you want to go that route.

You've got to remember that AFM started in the 80's,and arose primarily due to the rise of VHS. Much of the deal structure came out of people inventing it as they went along. At least according to some of the people who were around when it started. With that in mind, it's pretty impressive how well the categorization of these rights has held up.

THEATRICAL

This should be fairly clear. Theatrical rights are for the rights to release in theaters. Again, this is usually done by territory. Producer's reps may help with this domestically, but you will generally need a sales agent to sell it internationally. You'll also need a genre film with some good cast to get this out there.

HOME VIDEO/DVD/BLU-RAY

Believe it or not, there is still a market for DVD and Blu-ray. A lot of it is international, but there are still major retailers like Wal-Mart, Target, and occasionally Redbox who sales agents sell to domestically. Most often a sales agent will sell them to either a wholesaler or a representative from a major brand.

There are also outlets that can help you self-distribute those rights, and Ingram Entertainment will even allow you to sell to stores.

PAY TV

Pay TV is essentially Premium TV. These are places like HBO, Starz, Showtime, etc. These deals are generally exclusive and will often also include an SVOD license. This is so that the network can include the offering on their associated SVOD platforms and extensions.

For instance, this allows HBO to put the content on HBO Go and HBO Now. It also allows Starz to use the content on their Amazon Prime extension and Showtime to show your work on Hulu.

CABLE/NETWORK TV

As it would sound, Cable TV is for non-PayTV rights, and Network is for the major "over the air" networks. These would be ABC, NBC, Fox, and CBS. Cable TV channels are very similar to Network TV but are more restricted in terms of content. As such, they are still often subject to some degree of censorship in the case of R- Rated movies and are slightly less likely to seek SVOD rights, although many of them will still take that right. Generally, a sales agent will window these rights later on in the release of your project.

VOD

As I'm sure you already know, VOD stands for Video On Demand. What you may not know is that there's more than one type of Video on Demand Service and each type has different providers. Here's a very brief outline of what the different types of VOD rights are and some samples as to the people who provide that service.

PPVOD/TVOD

This stands for Pay Per Video On Demand or Transactional Video on Demand. This has largely replaced Pay Per View television rights and is generally the most accessible form of VOD. There are many platforms for PPVOD. I believe the most obvious would be iTunes, Google Play, Amazon/Createspace, and Vimeo On Demand.

My favorite of them by far is VHX. I personally recommend them to all of my clients and I use it myself for Producer Foundry. They offer all the functionality of Vimeo on Demand, in a much more streamlined way with fewer fees and few caps. Shortly before the second edition of this book was published, Vimeo Acquired VHX. It's not yet clear when or how that will effect VHX's offerings, but it will be interesting to see what unfolds.

SVOD

Subscription Video on Demand (SVOD) is for VOD platforms that run on a subscription basis. This would be platforms like Netflix, Hulu Plus, Fandor, as well as extensions of PayTV and regular TV channels as mentioned above.

ESP/ANCILLARY VOD

These are primarily independent ancillary VOD platforms. Ever order a film on the back of your seat on Virgin America or Atlantic? You just took part in an ESPVOD platform. Hotel Rights would also be considered ancillary VOD rights.

Cable TV producers often have their own PPVOD channels. If you've ever watched a movie on demand through Xfinity that would have been a ESPVOD transaction.

That said, sometimes there is some contention on these rights. Sometimes they'll just be included in PPVOD rights, so it's important to clarify. Generally, you have to be a US distributor in order to get your movie on these platforms. These are platforms that filmmakers can approach directly.

AVOD

The final type of VOD service is AVOD. This is Ad-supported on demand content. Youtube would technically fall into this category, but there are many more that do as well.

RIGHTS BY TERRITORY

So now that you have a good understanding of the media right types in an international distribution deal are, it's time to briefly go over what the territories for a sales agency agreement are. There is some variance depending on which sales agency you're talking to.

Generally territorial rights are broken down by region and then further sub-divided by territory. It's important to keep in mind these territories are grouped by language and demography just as much if not more than they are by geography.

On the next page you'll find a sample of how territories are generally broken down throughout the world. Most times, you'll find this sort of sheet attached as an appendix with high and low sales estimates on them. If a deal you're offered has that then it's generally a good sign.

Europe		English Speaking
Benlux		Australia
France		South Africa/Africa
Germany		United Kingdom
Greece		USA/Canada
Italy		**Latin America**
Portugal		Latin America All
Spain		Argentina/Paraguay/
Scandinavia		Uruguay/Chile/Peru
Russia CIS		Brazil
Far East		Mexico
Japan		**Other**
Hong Kong		Bulgaria
Indonesia		Czech Republic
Philippines		Romania
Malaysia		Poland
Singapore		Ex-Yugoslavia
South Korea		Israel
Taiwan		India
Thailand		Turkey
China		Middle East

CHAPTER 20 – THE FIVE WINDOWS OF DIY INDIEFILM DISTRIBUTION

Not every film is well suited for traditional distribution. Most sales agents have a saying for what they're looking for – "Bullets and Babes". So if you've made a film that doesn't fit the hot genres and doesn't have any notable talent, you're going to need to plan your distribution carefully. Luckily, there are tools that can help you make the most out of your DIY distribution. Here's a top-level view of them.

WINDOW 1: PROMOTE AND GET PARTNERS TO HELP YOU

Whether we're talking about traditional distribution or self-distribution, phase one is always to spread awareness of your film. It's generally best for this to start in the early stages of making your film. However, it's never too late to start promoting.

First seek out partners with expertise in traditional distribution, online marketing, and festival promotion. They can help you minimize costs and maximize your efficacy. They'll also help you build and engage with your community. The earlier you bring them on, the more effective they'll be.

Once your film is completed, you should start submitting to smaller festivals and those that fit whatever niche your film falls into. If you made a film about environmental issues, there are a lot of green film festivals, including the SF Green Film Festival. If you happen to be an Asian American there are festivals that were created for you as well, including CAAMfest. If you made an LGBTQ film, then there are quite a lot of festivals available to you. If you're in SF, the big fish is Frameline.

No matter what, make sure to submit to your local festivals. You can start a loyal fan base and grow hometown recognition by submitting to these festivals. Often, they're easier to get into, although this is less true if you're in San Francisco or another major hub. If you are, you might want to target the newer film festivals.

It's surprising how much good a hometown following can do for you. I still let the paper from the mountain town I grew up in know any time I do something big.

Smaller, local film festivals won't do much for you in terms of traditional distribution, though. The only ones that will are the top-tier festivals I.E. Cannes, Sundance, Toronto, Tribeca, and perhaps SXSW. If you can get into any of those, then your chances for traditional distribution go up substantially. Although, it's not likely you'll get in.

Feel free to submit to the next top-tier festival that's coming up. The submissions are not incredibly expensive and if you get in the career boost is substantial. Since they require premiere status, you might even want to hold back accepting a place in any of the other festivals. Although if you don't get into that closest upcoming top-tier film festival, don't wait for the next one.

Start taking festival spots. Once they're more than a year old, they're a lot harder to sell. Again, films are not evergreen.

WiINDOW 2: HIGH TOUCH PPVOD AND DVDs IN STORES

As soon as you get into a single festival, get your film on Ingram Entertainment, VHX, and Vimeo On Demand. There will be an up-front cost for most of those – potentially as much as $300-$500 all in.

That said, they're not available on as many platforms as accessible as something like iTunes or Google Play. Additionally they're not great about helping with marketing. But retaining the 90/10 split is much better to earn some money for the work you've put in to create your project.

VHX also lets you keep track of people who buy your video and even add their emails to your list which is fantastic for building your community.

Ingram Entertainment is a DVD wholesaler. It's the platform used by booksellers large and small, as well as many other brick and mortar content selling businesses. You'd be surprised where you end up with your content on Ingram. This book is an example of that. If you bought this book anywhere except Amazon or an event I hosted, produced, or spoke at, then it got there with the help of Ingram.

This window should be done concurrently with the first window. When your project gets into a festival, make sure to call local DVD retailers and bookstores to let them know that your film is in a local festival and they can get your DVD on Ingram. Make sure you include local stores with your DVD on your handouts, as well as the VHX and Vimeo URLs. You'd be surprised what support and sales you can drum up. You could include a QR code, but hardly anyone uses them.

WINDOW 3 – BROAD PPVOD

About 6 months after your initial VOD release, towards the end of your festival run you should consider hiring an aggregator and getting your film on iTunes and Google Play. Depending on which aggregator you use, you may want to do Createspace yourself, since it's relatively easy.

It's nearly impossible to get on iTunes without an Aggregator. You'll want to pick your aggregator carefully, since some of them will have connections to get you on Amazon Prime, Hulu, and occasionally Netflix. Although Amazon Prime is easier, now that they've opened up access.

Make sure you do your research on aggregators, and understand what they charge. There are some articles and price quotes in the resource packet at TheGuerrillaRep.com.

WINDOW 4 — SVOD

After about 6-9 months, it's time to boost your brand by getting your film on Netflix, Amazon Prime, Hulu, Fandor (my favorite) and some others. You won't get much money for this, but you will get a lot of visibility.

For all of those except perhaps Amazon Prime and Fandor, you'll need connections through an aggregator or a sales agent. Most of them don't take open submissions. Additionally, this is far from guaranteed; they generally only take 1 in 10 of the films they're pitched.

The real point of this is to build your brand for your next film. If you want to build to something better, telling investors your last film is on Netflix helps them understand that you are experienced and tested.

WINDOW 5 — LOSS LEADER

Once your licenses expire from the SVOD period, you should consider giving the film away for free on your website. This window is likely to be 3–4 years after release. I recommend doing this behind an email capture wall. You could use Youtube as a way to drive traffic to the email capture. You could also use Vimeo or VHX to help with delivery.

Giving away streams in exchange for email addresses can help you build a following and grow your audience so you can crowdfund your next project.

SECTION 4: THE CHANGING FACE OF INDEPENDENT FILM AND ADVICE FROM DISTRIBUTORS, SALES AGENTS AND FINANCIERS

CHAPTER 21 – HOW IS AFM AND THE INDUSTRY CHANGING?

Since the first edition of this book, the American Film Market has changed in some small but significant ways. It has had to adapt to keep up with changes in the industry as a whole. In an interview with Jonathan Wolf (Managing Director of the American Film Market) I did for HopeForFilm.com, he said the following:

"Technology has always influenced film. Filmmaking was made possible because of a technology invented by Edison and tech will continue to shape the industry, just as technology influences every industry."

THE CHANGING FACE OF CONTENT DELIVERY

As stated previously, AFM and other markets came to prominence out of a need to sell the rights for VHS replication. Given the novelty of being able to watch a movie, you could charge a shocking amount of money for a cassette in the early days of home video. As more content entered the market, the price point dropped.

Then DVD entered the market. If you owned a professional DVD replicator in the early days, you could build a business amazingly fast. Some companies arose overnight by printing early content from the public domain to get their early capital. Shortly thereafter, they started buying up catalog rights and printing DVDs. Many companies rose to prominence doing exactly that.

It was not too long ago that SVOD rights were something that filmmakers just got to keep since they had no real value. While the rise of Amazon Prime and Netflix added some value to those rights, the licensing rights were not always as great as we could hope. That is, unless you were producing one of their original series.

The big game changer for SVOD has been HBO launching HBO Now. While HBO had the service HBO Go which was offered as a free add-on to their cable subscription package, their move into Over the Top Services (OTT) predicates a substantial shift in where the general industry is heading. Now most PayTV channels have subscription services that can be offered as add-ons to other services like Hulu Plus and Amazon Prime. Because of this, the value of SVOD rights have changed drastically.

Given that the VOD market is shifting towards subscriptions for content, the ability to sell single licenses has diminished greatly. Not too many people buy DVDs when they can find what they need on Netflix. It can be done, but the sales tactics have changed and the filmmaker needs to be more involved in promoting their own work.

A similar thing happened in the publishing industry about a decade ago, then it was loosely mirrored by disruption in the music industry. Authors tend to make their money from speaking and consulting, and musicians make their money from shows. It is unclear what exactly filmmakers will use to replace the lost income down the road, so right now we're still reliant on older methods to grow our audience and grow our income.

AFM and markets like it are and will continue to be the best, most cost-effective way to establish relationships with people who can take your content wider and build your brand so you can actually make a career doing what you love.

I advocate a hybrid system. You should keep some of your rights to handle on your own and let a distributor or sales agent sell the rights you couldn't. If you can couple that and the other methods and tactics mentioned in the previous chapter, then you can use the market to grow your filmmaking career.

THE GROWING IMPORTANCE OF NICHE MARKETS

If you are looking to grow your filmmaking career, one of the best ways to do so is to target a niche audience or community. Before I go into some examples, I will say one thing: whatever niche audience you choose to target, the film you make must be authentic. If it's not, then the demographic will feel pandered to, and like you're only trying to take their money.

Faith-based films have been growing exponentially since the first publication of this book. If you happen to have a passion for faith-based films, then making one is a great route in to making a very good living as a professional filmmaker.

I have some friends who distribute faith based films. Every them I talk to them they've grown their business in impressive ways. Have a built in audience that's hungry for content. If you can couple that with the growing need for family content, then it can lead to a very lucrative career creating the films and projects you love.

It's important to not enter this niche solely for the money. As mentioned previously, no one will want to consume this content if it is inauthentic. If you're working within the faith-based demographic, you generally have to be a person of faith yourself. They tend to not be so kind to people who don't share their beliefs but want to create content for them.

Unfortunately, once you get into the faith-based film industry, it can be very difficult to break out. Much of your audience will not follow you outside of the faith-based genre, so you'll be largely starting from scratch. This is true of all niche markets, but it is particularly true of faith-based market.

Another entrenched and underserved niche demographic is the LGBT market. The LGBT demographic is also very hungry for high-quality content that speaks to their needs and their life experience. There is also a strong need for family content in the LGBT community, since many LGBTQ families are adopting children or using surrogates. This niche is one that really needs filling, as these families have a strong need to feel normalized.

This demographic mirrors the faith-based demographic in some surprising ways. The most important being that this content cannot be perceived to be pandering. For this community, content must be authentic.

That said, unlike the faith-based community, you don't have to be a full-fledged member of the LGBT community in order to make content for them. You have to have spent time in the community and you have to be accepting and non-judgmental, but if you can make an authentic LGBT movie as a straight person, you can still develop an audience and a following.

There are plenty of other niches you could target. Goths, bowlers, techies, families with children with disabilities, runners, bicyclists, office workers, retail workers, restaurant workers – I could go on for quite a while. Just think of any niches that need content they can relate to. Any way people identify whether by choice or not by choice. If it happens to be a rather large demographic, then that's even better.

I understand I may sound callous breaking people into those sorts of groups. Keep in mind, your end goal is to create high-quality content that speaks to people. You want people to watch your film and gain a better understanding of themselves, someone they know, or the world around them. You're creating something that can be used to comfort someone and communicate something about them that mere words often cannot.

THE FILM BUSINESS IS INCREASINGLY INTERNATIONAL

Unsurprisingly, the business of international sales has always been global. However, in the past five or so years, the industry has become even more globalized. Many new territories are either emerging or growing and domestic revenues are either remaining stagnant, or decreasing.

Asia's importance as a territory is growing in a huge way. As anyone paying attention should know, China's economic boom has created a growing need for content within the country. In fact, China's box office has outpaced America's for a few weekends. That's the only time that has ever happened in the history of theater-going. These are not the only indicators of the growing importance of China as a territory.

In 2014 by the numbers, buyers from Asia represented 30.7% of total buyers, and 28.3% of total buyer companies attending AFM. This is more than any other continent, with the exception of Europe. However Europe is generally broken into EU and non-EU territories, and when taken individually those are both less than Asia.

Also in 2014 China had particularly strong growth in attendance, with a 40% growth in total buyers and a 19% growth in buying companies attending the show. So not only are more companies attending AFM, but the companies that have already been attending are growing. This is unsurprising given the economic growth and spike in demand across the country.

While Asia and China should not be surprising to anyone reading this book, it may be surprising to learn about the growth of Latin America as a whole, and Brazil in particular.

The number of Brazilian buyers attending the show in 2014 doubled. The number of individual buyers was up from twenty buyers from nine companies in 2013 to forty buyers from fifteen companies in 2014.

However it should be noted that this does not necessarily indicate a shift in buying power. AFM only tracks the number of attendees, not the total number of films they buy. So one buyer from Australia could quite possibly buy as much media as 10 from Brazil.

There are many more trends that indicate a larger shift within the film industry. Unfortunately, those will have to wait for future blogs or perhaps a different book.

CHAPTER 22 – THE CHANGING FACE OF FILM FINANCING AND PRESALES

Technology is shaping not only the content delivery side, but also helping to change the face of film financing. In the past few years, several platforms have come to prominence that dramatically changed the face of film financing, marketing, and distribution.

TECHNOLOGY AND INVESTMENT

Slated has become much more of a player for independent film investment than they were when the first edition of this book was published. Slated is a platform that helps filmmakers connect with investors. The company is modeled around a software company called AngelList. The founder of Slated – Stephan Paternot – was also an early investor in AngelList. The idea behind it was to better enumerate the value of a package based on previous credits, as well as market reach and viability.

While it's not necessarily a great place to find equity investment, it can help filmmakers to complete their financial mix with gap debt. It's also an interesting option if you would want to approach lower-interest, presale-backed debt.

THE EMERGENCE OF CROWDFUNDING

Crowdfunding is here to stay, particularly as more and more content is being created. If you properly utilize your tools to grow and stay engaged with your audience, crowdfunding can be a fantastic way to continually finance your content. There are more ways to do that than simply putting your project up on Kickstarter or Indiegogo.

Crowdfunding may be a lot of work, but it is worth it. If you're using rewards-based crowdfuning, it can be a way for you to pre-sell content directly to your fan base. Doing so can prove your market viability, and raise some of the money you need for your project without giving up any equity.

Patreon is a good way to make some money on an ongoing basis from a loyal fan following. It integrates well with YouTube and several other platforms, and can help you continue to build your skills and career with some stable income derived from your content.

However, for more project-based crowd funding, Seed & Spark can be an excellent platform for filmmakers. It was designed by and built for the needs of media creators. They can even help you distribute your project when you're done.

There's even a new trend of equity based crowd funding that's been enabled by the JOBS act. This would enable you to sell shares in your project through a third-party service that can help your fans truly be a part of your movie.

If your fans own a piece of your film, there's a good chance they will fund it even more than they otherwise would. Once the film gets out there, they'll also be more likely to promote it.

PRESALES ARE ALIVE AND WELL AT AFM

Surprising, right? Everything you read says that presales are a dying business, but according to AFM's Managing Director Jonathan Wolf, about 60% of the business done at this year's AFM was in presales. This means more than half a billion USD in presales alone.

According to Mr. Wolf, the market for foreign presales came back by 2010 or 2011. The biggest reason for the initial decline was the glut of equity financing that entered during the economic boom that preceded the 2008 recession.

Presale financing has an enhanced degree of risk and the biggest reason most buyers take the risk is the fact that they can get the content they need for their distribution platforms.

However, given how many films were being made, the price for finished films began to drop due to the abundance of similar films and filmmakers needing to get something for their projects. Since there was such an abundance of content, buyers were far more likely to have options to find what they needed and fill their quotas without having to pay for presale. With that, as well as the inherent risk involved in buying something before you can see it, the presale market dried up.

When the recession hit the equity dried up and fewer films were being made, so the market shifted from being a buyer's market to more of a balanced market. So presales became viable again.

That said, it's not an easy business to be in. It's only really viable for films over $500K in particular genres, with some talent or at least a tested franchise, and a tested director. Without those factors, the glut of content still exists due to the lowered barrier to entry to make a film. Rich Klubeck, a partner at UTA (United Talent Agency said the following at the finance conference: "A lot of the best movies are execution-dependent, and that means presales are just not viable."

Dramas just aren't pre-sellable because even with the best script, talent, and director, there's no real way to tell whether the film will be sellable to a wide audience. A film like *Expendables 4* or *Sharknado 3* is going to be sellable in many markets regardless of execution. However, a film like *Brokeback Mountain* or *Her* might not be sellable, depending on its execution.

According to the finance conference, while presales have come back, they've taken a little bit of a different form. Instead of letters of credit directly from international buyers being taken to banks and backed to finance part of the film, reputable sales agents are issuing MGs at an earlier stage that can be taken to the bank. Keep in mind that not all sales agents at AFM would be considered reputable enough for a bank to back the presale on letter of credit alone.

If you want to find out which ones would be, the best course of action would be to talk to some of the banks providing presale-backed loans in their Los Angeles branches.

CHAPTER 23 – WHAT DISTRIBUTORS AND SALES AGENTS WANT

This book is written primarily for filmmakers to learn the ins and outs of the American Film Market and to give advice on how you can find distribution at the market. While I've been going to the market for six years and learned a lot, I've only been repping films for other people's projects for about half of that time. In my time at AFM, I have met a lot of distributors and financiers who have been in the game far longer than I have, so I sent several of them an email asking what advice they had for filmmakers new to attending AFM. (Bolding is mine)

I asked these questions:

1. What's the first thing you look for when a filmmaker approaches you about distribution?

2. What advice would you give a filmmaker friend attending AFM for the first time?

3. What has a filmmaker done to make you never want to do business with them?

I'm including the responses I got from distributors and sales agents who said they don't mind being quoted in this chapter. These emails have been edited for grammar and spelling, but the content has not been changed.

Daisy Hamilton
Head of Business Development & Acquisitions
TriCoast Worldwide

1. What's the first thing you look for when a filmmaker approaches you about distribution?

-Elements already in place (cast/director/financing)

-This is essential; there are literally millions of people with great ideas or great scripts. Only a handful have a project ready and able to go into pre-production or production. It also helps find those few capable of execution.

-Furthermore, when a producer approaches us with a package, no matter how great the story is, if there are no elements in place, they are basically obligating us to act as producers. If we are going to start from scratch and act as producers, it will be on projects we develop in-house.

-Equity committed and equity needed

-We want to see there are already some funds in place. The first piece of the pie is always the hardest to get. For good producers this isn't an issue. We rarely, if ever, put "first money in" and we would never invest in a filmmaker we've never worked with before.

-Genre

-Dramas are a no. This is only because we are international sales agents/distributors and not domestic. Dramas do not get exported, as countries prefer watching their own dramas. It also has to do with government subsidies on the international side.

-Presale viability

-Assuming it's a project with some attachments and assuming there is already some equity in place, the next most important thing is the director. If it is a first-time director, pre-sales are ABSOLUTELY out of the question. International buyers require the financial performance of the director's previous films before they will even consider a presale.

-All that said, at the heart of it, the very first thing I look for is personality, charisma, and magnetism. These qualities can be found in the majority of successful producers. I want someone I can perceive as a good partner, because at the end of the day, producers become our partners when we go to sell the film. Working with people who have a bad attitude makes my job less enjoyable. Luckily, the reverse is also true.

2. What advice would you give a filmmaker friend attending AFM for the first time?

-Make Friends. Create relationships that can last beyond the market. Build friendships that have a genuine foundation beyond just what you can get from them. Find ways of offering people something they don't already have. If a filmmaker doesn't have the resources to offer an attractive package, the only other reason anyone would want to get into business with him/her is because he or she is an awesome human being that people genuinely want to work with.

3. What has a filmmaker done to make you never want to do business with them?

-Oy vey – where to start. I've been literally stalked and harassed at AFM. It's worse than any other market I attend, probably because AFM is in LA and doesn't cost as much as a trip to Cannes would. Thus people not in the film world and not familiar with film business etiquette all congregate in the downstairs bar and/or the outside smoking area. If a person approaches me and starts pitching without first perceiving or verbally asking if I'm willing/wanting to hear their pitch, the chances I'd work with them are slim to none, no matter what the content of their pitch is.

Markets are incredibly busy for distributors and sales agents; this is where we make money for our producers! I genuinely believe AFM is a great place to meet new producers and create relationships, but it's not the place to acquire new projects in development. That happens after the market, once we've closed enough deals to be able to invest in a new film. From our perspective, the first priority is definitely not films in development. Selling is first, acquiring finished films is second, and third would be creating relationships (buyers/agents/producers etc.)

Chris Hood
CEO
Robin Hood Films

1. What's the first thing you look for when a filmmaker approaches you about distribution?

Name talent and genre – Since we handle mostly smaller films, we don't really see much "A-list" talent, but there are plenty of smaller names that aid a film, especially in international markets. Genre is the other important factor. I can sell a bad zombie film far easier than a great drama. Comedy is a terrible genre to try to sell internationally, as are documentaries.

2. What advice would you give a filmmaker friend attending AFM for the first time?

My first piece of advice would actually be don't try getting distribution at the AFM. Distributors are there to sell movies, not pick them up. Even when a good film walks in the door, my first thought is "I wish they'd reached out to me three months ago. I would be selling the film at this market". I suppose if your film was just finished before the market, it's an okay idea, but sitting on your film to wait for the AFM is a terrible idea. Sure, all the distributors are there in one place, but you can get a list or find out who they are without waiting for the market. You may think it's convenient for you to have them all there in person, but the reality is – distributors are at the AFM to sell, not acquire. The months leading up to the market are the time they're trying to find films. Many, if not most, companies don't even want to talk to people with projects since their focus is sales that week. The bigger companies intentionally don't have their acquisitions people attend for this very reason.

Don't show up at the AFM with a film partially finished trying to create "buzz". If you have a big film with A-list talent, you can try this, but you still won't get a lot of mileage. You're not going to sell the film based on a trailer, so what you're really doing is generating waning interest you can't deliver on in a timely fashion. If I see a great trailer, I want to see the film right away. If the screener rolls in three months later, much of the excitement is gone.

Finally, don't come to the AFM trying to raise money for a film project unless it's a stellar package. By that, I mean you have a great project in a marketable genre with some of the following: A) most of the funding already in place, B) presales, C) notable talent attached. Again, we're not at the AFM looking for scripts to produce. Even companies like ours that produce and co-produce aren't excited about having writers walk in with a finished script. Believe it or not, it's not that rare of an occurrence. Now, if you can walk in with a package including some money already committed and Jean-Claude Van Damme attached, that's something I'm interested in taking a look at.

3. What has a filmmaker done to make you never want to do business with them?

Evidencing their cluelessness as to the business of film. Most filmmakers who call, write, or walk through the door at the AFM simply have no business making films. It's frustrating and sad at the same time that, for most of these people, they've been working toward this dream for a very long time and failed miserably for inexcusable reasons. People come in with films that completely miss the mark; the genre is bad, the trailer is bad, the poster is awful, the casting is tragic and/or they have nothing remotely close to a realistic expectation. A $100K film isn't going to get a $100K advance. A $500K film that doesn't have a name any bigger than Martin Kove or Adrian Paul is going to be a failure financially. I often learn in the first two minutes that the filmmaker falls into the group of people arrogantly tainting the entire business. The reason film is perceived as such a risky investment is because it is. And the reason it is, is simply because too many people are making films who shouldn't be. So these fools do frustrate me, but at the same time, I do sympathize because I'm witnessing the death of a dream. Everyone loses.

Hmm, seems I went off on a bit of a tangent.

It may also interest your readers to know that I have a blog at MovieIndustry.com about filmmaking that might provide some more insight into my thoughts.

Steve Arroyave
CEO
Arrow Entertainment

1. What's the first thing you look for when a filmmaker approaches you about distribution?

Arrow Entertainment is currently focused on theatrical biopics, true stories, and socially conscious films and we are therefore looking for projects that fit these criteria. One of the first questions I ask filmmakers is who specifically is the audience for their film. Often they come back with something like "this is a film for everyone" or "this is a woman's film" or "this is for young males", but this is too vague for me. I then ask them to imagine that they had to market the film to their audience and how would they go about doing it and specifically which groups of people would be interested in their film and how you would reach them. If they can't answer this question, then likely neither can we. Nor can the distributors we sell to.

2. What advice would you give a filmmaker friend attending AFM for the first time?

Find companies that focus on the same kind of project they are looking to get made.

3. What has a filmmaker done to make you never want to do business with them?

Pretend to know more than they know.

Annick Mahnert
Acquisitions Consultant
Screen Division

1. What's the first thing you look for when a filmmaker approaches you about distribution?

It all depends on the project and where it stands development-wise. If it's only a script, I'd like to know if it's in financing and if someone is already attached to it.

Usually, it becomes interesting if a producer is attached. I look at their previous work (short films, other productions) and this will help weight a project.

2. What advice would you give a filmmaker friend attending AFM for the first time?

This is a very difficult question. The AFM is foremost a market. Main attendees are distributors from around the world who want to buy from sales agents. You may set up meetings with sales agents if you think you have a product that might interest them, but make sure you check out their lineup first and don't waste their time. And if someone tells you he has no time or he's not interested, let it go and move on.

3. What has a filmmaker done to make you never want to do business with them?

The worst thing a filmmaker can do is approach me as if I were his friend and force something upon me – a script, a DVD... And, same as the previous question: I receive a lot of email from filmmakers who absolutely have no idea who I am and what I am looking for. If you approach someone or a company, make sure first that you check out who they are, target the ones who think might fit your project. And don't harass them afterwards.

Jude Tucker
Founder and CEO
FilmFunder.com

1. What's the first thing you look for when a filmmaker approaches you about distribution?

I am primarily involved in the finance side of motion pictures. I look for projects that have distribution, presales, or a very good chance at getting presales. When a producer pitches a project to me, I really care about the full picture (story, genre, budget, who's in it, who's directing, who the DP is, etc.).

2. What advice would you give a filmmaker friend attending AFM for the first time?

If I were telling someone about AFM for the first time, I would make sure they go with a specific plan regarding their film and how to SELL IT. These distributors are not looking for the next artistic wonder-piece; they are looking for a movie that will SELL UNITS. So show them something that will prove that your movie will sell units. A mock poster that looks really badass and has great actor names (even if they are not contractual) goes a long way.

3. What has a filmmaker done to make you never want to do business with them?

My two biggest pet peeves are when a producer presents a budget that is either A) ridiculous for the project they are trying to make (like spending 5 million on a horror movie with no names in it. That film should be made for less than $200K. Come on. Or B) Ridiculous for that producer's experience level (aka a producer who has a ton of short films and $200K horror films suddenly thinks he is equipped to handle a $5MM union tier II project. No Way.

Most of my 38 feature films have been in the budget range of $300K - $1.5M. It's a really comfortable range for me and I don't really like to venture out of it because it's what I know and do so well.

Phil Gorn
CEO
Wonderphil Entertainment

1. What's the first thing you look for when a filmmaker approaches you about distribution?

Film, trailer, poster (in that order). With the market harder than ever, distributors are looking at the entire film more closely (as opposed to skimming through, viewing the trailer and poster, and giving a green light).

2. What advice would you give a filmmaker friend attending AFM for the first time?

Have your one-sentence pitch as tight as possible. Then have your long pitch ready if someone wants to hear more. And remember that it's better to show one minute of good footage, then several minutes of footage that isn't ready. Pique the person's interest so they are asking for more.

3. What has a filmmaker done to make you never want to do business with them?

Lie. A small fib about the budget or something else is understandable but if a filmmaker treats me like the enemy and lies or goes behind my back then I'm done and will never respond to them again.

Al Perez de la Mesa
APM Entertainment, Inc.
President

1. What's the first thing you look for when a filmmaker approaches you about distribution?

Since I primarily deal with titles in post-production or that are completed, I look for the quality of the production and assess the characteristics of the film including the cast and crew, genre, script/storyline, editing, along with its promotability.

2. What advice would you give a filmmaker friend attending AFM for the first time?

Meet and assess the profiles of the various agents to determine their films and territories of specialty. Assess separating the rights by territory among different agents as well as separating the rights themselves versus a worldwide or an all-rights deal.

3. What has a filmmaker done to make you never want to do business with them again?

Making repetitive and abundant requests with an unrealistic time expectation of having it completed.

Tony Taglienti
Managing Director
4 Digital Media

1. What's the first thing you look for when a filmmaker approaches you about distribution?

I look at their poster or sales sheet to see if it sells me the film in a few seconds. If not, I look to see if the film might have a hook that would enable us to redesign the poster to appeal to our target audience in 2.8 seconds without anyone having to "sell" the film. The poster comes first, the film comes second.

2. What advice would you give a filmmaker friend attending AFM for the first time?

Listen, listen, listen, and learn. Talk to as many distributors and sales agents as possible to get a feel for the state of the market, what's working for them, and find out if your film appeals to its intended target audience.

3. What has a filmmaker done to make you never want to do business with them again?

Been too precious about changing the title of his film and his poster design when we have proven both are wrong for the market. Big egos don't sell films.

Author's Note
Given I'm a Producer's rep, I talk to sales agents and distributors on a more regular basis than I can iterate this book.

So I'll be adding more interviews to the resource packet on TheGuerrillaRep.com as they become available.

CHAPTER 24 – AN INTERVIEW WITH DAISY HAMILTON

During the research for this book I conducted an interview with Daisy Hamilton, VP of Acquisitions for Tricoast Worldwide. While pieces of this interview have been included throughout the book, I wanted to include a transcript of the interview so you could get the information straight from the horse's mouth. The interview has been edited for grammar, but the content has not been changed.

Ben: In terms of making a deal, which is more important: the film or the filmmaker?

Daisy: The filmmaker.

Ben: Could you elaborate?

Daisy: Well, I think both are really important. In order to make a good film, it has to be a project that every single person working on that film wants to do and everyone feels they are working on something greater than themselves. In order to do that you need a director who can catalyze a large group of people, bring them together, and steer that ship correctly. If you don't have that, it's just a great story with sloppy execution.

Ben: How important is the film director's passion for their film when you're dealing with them?

Daisy: I hate to say it but not that important at all. Everybody feels that they have a great script or a great project, and while passion is necessary and important, it's not a rare quality.

Ben: So what are the most important selling points for a film other than what you've already mentioned in your email?

Daisy: If we're talking about a producer, it would have to be their ability to create relationships and sustain those relationships. Whether it be with executives or on set, that is a producer's job. Also I think it's just as important that a producer be able to identify their audience, because there's no point in making a film if it doesn't have an audience. Then it's sort of <pause> self-indulgent.

Ben: How many screeners do you get on a weekly or monthly basis for a deal?

Daisy: There are two questions there. Sent to me unsolicited I get 1 or 2 a week, depending. If it's around AFM, I get a lot more. Then there are times, like before Cannes, where I went out and sought out films, and then those 3 or 4 come in. Usually, to be honest, the films that are sent to me are of a lower quality than the films I go out and seek to acquire. It's best when I already have a relationship with the producer. I can call him up and say, "Hey, I see you're making another film, let's start talking earlier rather than later".

Ben: How great a percentage of your catalogue is from repeat work with the same filmmakers?

Daisy: About 40%. Maybe 50%.

Ben: What do you do with the screeners you receive unsolicited?

Daisy: We have a 20-minute rule. If you don't know the point of the film within 20 minutes, if the production value is horrific, if it doesn't have a point yet, if it doesn't have an audience yet by the first 20 minutes we don't have to watch on. I send them an apologetic email.

Ben: What's the best way a filmmaker can approach you outside of the market?

Daisy: Well, I hate getting log lines in the mail. We don't work with scripts. If we're going to produce something we have tons of amazing scripts we've already developed in-house. I'm usually receptive to emails that are packages, like well put together pretty little power points or packets that identify the audience, give a synopsis, tell me the budget, what they already have in terms of money in place, and cast in place. Cast attachment is obviously preferred, obviously everyone sends pictures of their wish list, but how realistic is that? So I'm receptive to packages.

Phone calls are, honestly, fast, and if someone calls me, even if I'm busy I really will call them back. Or I'll just take a quick phone call and I'm usually pretty honest. If there are elements we can work with I'll sit there on the phone for 30 minutes and talk with them about the different options and if it's something I'm receptive to I'll have them send the script over. We want to know how we can help because we really become a producer's partner as distributor or as a sales agent — either one. That's an important difference where if a producer wants us to put down money on the film, then we're their distributor so we're actually their partners in it.

On the other hand, if we don't have to put down money and we're just acting as a sales agent we're still their partner in the sense that we're responsible for placing their film and allowing their film to recoup money. There's got to be a daily or weekly – more recently daily because of Cannes — but a dialogue about materials, deliverables; often times we have to position the film slightly differently than we would position it for a domestic audience.

International drama, for instance, it's just not exported. Countries prefer to buy their own dramas; they don't import dramas. So we have to find another way to position the film – maybe it's a dark comedy or there are a myriad of other ways we can make a drama seem like it's not a drama. We work with the filmmakers in a lot of different senses.

Also because we're an interesting company in that we have a full-fledged production house, we're able to take a package at different stages. Say a producer has some elements of soft money already in place; if it's a project we like and we see the potential in and the producer's done all of his leg work, we can look at coming in with post-production or presales if it's not a first-time director. So it's sort of like we can put all the final pieces together.

We also have really strong relationship with film commissioners around the world and I don't understand why American producers don't do everything within their power to take advantage of tax incentives. European producers get the majority – 90% if not 100% – of their movies funded by tax credits, and then every dollar they make is butter. Americans think it's cool to get a movie fully funded by equity, but I can't think of a more dangerous thing to do for investors.

Ben: Are there any other genres that should be avoided?

Daisy: Sports.

Ben: Sports?

Daisy: Yeah. Think about it. Baseball, that's really only America and Japan. So that's so limiting. Foreign sales should be 70% of a film's revenue if it's done properly. So you're immediately cutting out 70% of your profits.

Also, any kind of ethnic sub-culture should be avoided. I don't want to get myself in trouble for saying this, but if you look at an urban comedy or a Hispanic comedy they have huge domestic potential. HUGE, but they do not do well outside the US because those communities are not present around the world, so it's not content that is readily accessible to other countries.

That said, there are always films like "My Big Fat Greek Wedding", but I think that's because films like this, while they are about a specific culture's traditions, a lot of other cultures can really relate to it.

And if that's the case for an urban comedy, fantastic, but it just can't be using all inside jokes that are only accessible to the community that gets those inside jokes.

Also any comedies that are heavily language-based, you have to remember that in other countries the language is dubbed. You still have all your commonwealth countries to sell to, but if it's not a five-to-thirty-million dollar comedy with huge actors it's almost not worth the cost to dub for other countries.

Ben: How soon is too soon to seek a meeting with you at the market?

Daisy: It's my job to schedule the meetings with producers and we usually block them out the last two days. The first part of the market is absolutely for buyers. The producers who want to work with us should absolutely understand that because if they want us to be their sales agent or distributor at some point they're going to want us taking meetings with buyers.

Ben: How far in advance of the market should a filmmaker contact you?

Daisy: It's almost like it doesn't matter – what matters most is where they are with their package. If they just have a script, if they don't have money attached, if they don't have actors attached, it's just too early to meet with us. Better to come to us – it doesn't matter at what point in time – when they have a package that we can help them with. If it's too early then I'm just waiting for them to finish their legwork and it's more likely to just get lost in the many emails and business things going on.

That's why it's a time and a place thing. We had five countries call about two weeks ago in the ramp up for Cannes really wanting family films – anything with a dog or an animal. It could be completed – that would be awesome – but even if it were in preproduction they would be willing to buy. There was such a gap in family films that were being made. Countries really needed family films. We didn't have any completed ones so I immediately needed to look through all my emails, then I hit up all the producers that I know who are working on something like that. That's the thing where even if they don't have all the money in place we need this kind of content; there's a need for it. We have presales waiting and we'll help them get a great director, get a great cast, and then start getting the pre-sales immediately after.

At that point what's important is having a relationship with someone. That's the only time we'll seek out something that is early in development. Other than that, that's what a producer's job is. It's really separate jobs — the producer versus the distributor/sales agent. That's not to say we don't like getting involved earlier on; it's just to say there's a responsibility for the producer, and a different responsibility for the distributor/sales agent.

Ben: How long does it generally take a deal to go from the point where you've seen the screener to the point where you've closed the deal and it's in your market slate?

Daisy: It depends. In the weeks ramping up to Cannes I needed films — I needed at least two or three. Two great films were what I was trying to find, so I called everyone. If you lived in this town and you even thought about making a film I called you. I was not having much luck. Then in an hour on one Friday all of a sudden I had nine films to screen by the end of the day. I would say of those nine, five were great so we went after them and I ended up getting four because we were gearing up for Cannes.

There are different levels. First, there are the conversations, and then it's just us courting the producers. Then if they like us and we like them, we decide to work together. Then it's agreeing on deal points and usually we send them deal points or estimates before they agree to go with us and that's how we get the film.

Then it goes into long form and it can take anywhere from a week to two weeks, although I literally had a film last week that in two hours we had the deal signed. It was a Friday afternoon and we had the deal signed on Monday, because we needed to have all the materials so we could do the email blast for Cannes. We needed to get their film placed, so it was a timing thing in preparation for Cannes, but that was obviously on the quick side.

But I've also seen ... in one of the films we bought I'd been talking to them, trying to get this film for three months. It wasn't ready, but we had been courting them – dancing, I'd say, for three months. But I'd say on average it takes about two weeks.

Ben: How long after acquisition does it generally take for filmmakers to see revenue?

That's a good question because filmmakers need to know this. Most revenue comes in through the markets. It doesn't happen all at once; the revenue isn't generated in the first market. It takes at least the first year doing all the markets to make maybe 60% of the film's revenue back, if it's going to perform. Oftentimes it can be up to two years before all the money is recouped. If after two years ... we write these contracts in terms, so we have the first term we're on (in terms of a company we're on the really generous side), we will say if after eighteen months we're not able to recoup at least 75-100% of a film's budget, the filmmakers get their film back.

If after eighteen months we're not able to recoup 20% of the film's budget then you know we're not going to make it back. But if we do recoup it, then we extend to term 2, which is usually five years. So that's really important. I say this because honestly, I think it's so screwed up how many sales agents take advantage of filmmakers. I had a friend of mine who called me and said, "Hey, this sales agent wants my film". This film was made for $50-100K, [and] had some up and coming TV stars. The sales agent didn't want to put up any minimum guarantee. Which is fine; it's not great, but its not a very sought-after property. But they wanted it for thirty years, with no clauses for performance. That's just not fair.

Ben: That's insane!

Daisy: Yeah! It's not uncommon, though. And this wasn't a particularly well-known distributor. And what's worse is this distributor didn't go to any of the major markets. They put it through a secondary sales agent to represent at the market, so that's another hand-out. So this film, it's made for $50-100K, and they're not going to get theatrical. They're probably not going to get TV. They might get VOD, which doesn't pay advances, so with all these handouts the producer is giving away his film with zero chance to make anything more than pennies, ever.

If they had the performance clause in there they'd be in a way better position. This is not advantageous for me to say as a sales agent, but if we're unable to make TV or VOD sales after eighteen months, I think the producer should be the ones to put it on iTunes. Obviously there won't be marketing money behind it, but if we weren't able to do our jobs, why should we be getting that revenue?

That said, we do invest in each film, even if we're not giving them a minimum guarantee. The cost to go to a market is huge. Just to give you a snapshot for Cannes, for a company our size — midlevel but on our way up — it can be $250K per market. Just to attend Cannes, to do all the marketing, to meet with buyers, do screenings, do advertisings, do key art, do posters, do catalogues, do screeners, all of that. There's so much money that we as producers, as sales agents, have to put up. That's why in each contract you won't find a sales agent that doesn't have a marketing spend in it. A producer doesn't recoup money until the marketing is recouped; there are legitimate fees.

What's hard is sometimes we'll put in $50K for marketing and not make enough sales to recoup our marketing ... but if we're going to take that film to another market, then what? We just had an office meeting about this because there are films we're taking to market where we had already spent our marketing recoupment maximum. So any additional market we take them to is an additional investment on our part. So it's tricky. As sales agents we're assuming a lot of costs that producers don't necessarily realize or take into account. I don't know how I got to that from your question, but it's another point filmmakers and producers should be aware of.

Ben: It was all useful information. Here's my last question:

If a filmmaker sees you having drinks in the lobby after close, is it appropriate for them to approach you and try to have a conversation? Not to start pitching you immediately, but actually talk to you?

Daisy: Yes, I will say I am only receptive to pitches when it's somebody that I am enjoying being around. If I'm enjoying being in their presence at the moment, if they are [a] cool person and they seem like they are genuinely interested in making a friendship, or we have shared interests or we're getting along ... if they're good at schmoozing. I would say the best is when producers say, "Maybe we could schedule a meeting later" and then still want to talk and hang out and be my friend and whatever. That's cool.

That shows me they're really interested in creating a relationship. I'm honestly most-interested in working with producers I can have a good working relationship with. I'm interested in working with friends so I would think for a producer the best effort is to create a friendship first. When that friendship is created I'm willing to take far more steps to try to get a project made. At that point, I am then willing to look at a script that has no money, that has no actors and say, "Okay then, what can we do to get this made?" Then they're friends and I want to work with them. If they're not, then I just don't want to see their script – then they need to do their job as a producer before they come to me.

So I'm most receptive to pitches from people who are – or who may become – friends. Not only that – if they can create a real friendship I'd want to get my CEO's in a meeting, because I think these people are cool. I think it would be advantageous for our company to work with them. So then there's more chance that it's a meeting that has legs to it, so to speak.

This gets into something that's a little more difficult to refine and certainly can be hard for people to self-reflect on. I think it has to do with the difference between "I want to make a film for the first time" and "I'm a legitimate producer trying to make a career out of making films". I'm more interested in "Here's one film that I feel passionate about, but this is how I make my income. I'm a producer" because I find there are a lot of people that have a passion project that is one film.

If you have just one film you want to get made, bring on a seasoned person who is a producer. That is the best thing they can do to get it made. Not try to obligate the sales agent or the distributor and not try to start a conversation that actually isn't going to be fruitful for either party. It would be so much better for this person with the passion project to get hooked up with a great producer that can help them create an awesome package and then that producer can hit up me and all the other sales agents they are friends with.

Then it really can go somewhere as opposed to just stagnating. In that sense, I find most producers who are making a living from producing know it's way more advantageous to create a friendship and relationship with someone like my company or other companies. It's the people that are just doing a passion project that tend to really not understand the formalities and the etiquette of the market.

There is a business protocol to this, and not following those protocols can be really harassing and really abrasive. Part of the reason we have a booth person is to see our buyers, but really we have one to keep those kinds of producers out of our hair. In a market setting we're really focused on doing our job, so it can be distracting. There are so many other professions where you would not be allowed to get a meeting with someone if you're not qualified to take that meeting.

I don't know why it's so acceptable in film, and especially at AFM. Probably because you don't need to buy a thousand dollar plane ticket to get to Cannes so people just come out of the woodwork. It's hard to ask a producer to self-reflect on whether they think they're upholding correct business protocol. There definitely is a protocol and it's different to every other business. I think it's because it's not as corporate. It's not the same kind of corporate environment so people think, "Oh yeah, it's more laid back and you can be cool and unprofessional".

That's really not the case. There is definitely a level of etiquette that needs to be upheld and while it's different from corporate etiquette, and it's definitely based on networking and who you know, so that's important too. If there's a mutual friend, then immediately I'm more receptive than if there wasn't. I know that's hard, but if there is no mutual connection a person just needs to be able to start a genuine friendship. If they can't, they should team up with a producer that can. That's what a producer should be good at. So if they aren't, it would behoove them to know what their weaknesses are and bring somebody else onto their team that doesn't have those weaknesses. Because there are tons of people out there that are really great at making friendships.

Ben: That's actually part of the reason I've moved more from producing to producer's repping. Just the fact that my biggest skill set is schmoozing and making films is kind of secondary.

Daisy: I actually love people like you. This is too perfect. Sometimes a producer's rep will really try to get a[n] MG, because that's what's paying them. The film that I acquired in two hours, this filmmaker knew we really needed to place it before Cannes. She really wanted [an] MG. I didn't think it was worth an MG. She said something like "well we have other offers so we're just giving you one last chance to make an offer".

I said, "Listen, I'm not doing an MG, I don't need it. It's not something we'll pay an MG for. If those other offers fall through give me a call". In 20 minutes I got a call. And so I said to [her], "What can I do to make you get what you need, because I know without getting an MG you're not getting paid. So how about if I give you 5% of our take? We'll take 23% and 5% will go to you, and that would solve the issue that we're not paying an MG". [Sh]e still needed to get it placed, so we were able to make the deal and meet everyone's needs.

So sometimes I'll find the producer's reps will be asking for an MG when it's not really valid for the film. If it's valid for the film absolutely they should be asking for an MG, and it would be up to the producer's rep to really be able to analyze the project and say, "Is this something a sales agent should be paying money for? Should they be putting in an advance?"

That really has to do with the competition, or sometimes there's more to lose on the producer's side when we pay an MG. Once we're paying an MG everything else is stacked in our favor. I would say a producer will get so much more on the back end long term if we're not paying an MG. If we are, then that's just how the contract goes. We're putting up money; we are almost taking an equity position.

Well, we're not, but it also depends on the level of money that we are putting up. If we're putting up an advance, I would always recommend for a producer – if they believe in their film and they believe they'll get back end – don't ask for an advance. If you do, you're going to see your advance and then you're going to see a small amount of back end.

But of course, it just depends on how good the film is and whether it has elements that make it attractive for a sales agent. I love producer's reps. They really make our job easier.

Ben: That's all [of] my questions; is there anything else you'd like to add?

Daisy: There is something else I really hope gets in your book. I say this being a creative person in the film industry. I think that the function of stories has been lost a little bit in the effort to make money. Everyone feels they have a story to tell, but nobody looks at the stories that need to be told.

In that, I think directors and filmmakers have a responsibility. I take seriously the impact that sound and color can have on the psyche. People should know – or at least take into account – how their content is going to be affecting audiences on a subconscious level. It breaks my heart to see so many films exploiting women – exploiting the human body. It's telling, and it's sadder that there's such an appetite for that. The number of movies that make people laugh or inspire people or are really evocative is dwindling and people are just making these films because they have a small amount of money and they want to break into the film industry. They're not seizing the opportunity to make art and to create something that has a lasting impact on people.

That's the kind of films we need. That's what makes people excited. I would challenge people to get out of themselves and really start thinking about their audiences, and that goes into making money. If you know that if you are making a film that there's an appetite for, it really ... puts you in a better position. If your goal is to expand the consciousness or to involve the psyche in some way – that could be through fear, that could be through comedy, that could be through catharsis – what it's through doesn't matter. The point should be to evolve your audience in some way. It shouldn't be to waste their time. Why would any country want to buy that? Why would any audience want to buy that? It's important we don't do that.

I would challenge filmmakers to look at their content and really ask, "Is this helping the audience and is it worth their money?" Filmmaking should be a noble craft; it should be a noble thing. It's kind of sad that it often isn't anymore.

AFTERWORD

First of all, thank you for reading this book. I hope it's been helpful and that you now have a better understanding of how AFM works, and what it takes to find success there. I cannot recommend the resource packet at TheGuerrillaRep.com/Resources highly enough.

If you have any questions, comments, would like me to consider repping your film, would like to hire me as a consultant, or would like me to speak for your organization, feel free to reach out to me via TheGuerrillaRep.com or on Twitter. My Twitter Handle is @TheGuerrillaRep, and I'm pretty active so feel free to tweet me.

If you want more musings and advice on the film industry, you can find my blog on TheGuerillaRep.com. You can also find me on Facebook at Facebook.com/BenYennie. I generally only add people I know to my profile, but I post to my page regularly and you can contact me through there. Or if you don't feel like remembering all of this, you can find links to everything at about.me/benyennie. Also, if you genuinely liked the book, like the facebook page! You'll get updates on blogs, new editions, and other fun and useful stuff. Go to Facebook.com/TheGuerrillaRep.

ACKNOWLEDGEMENTS

As I said in the first edition, no one writes a book alone. I have been fortunate enough to learn from many great filmmakers, lawyers, sales agents, distributors, producer's reps, in my time at the IIFF, Global Film Ventures, and the Producer Foundry. Additionally there are the dozens of people who have offered advice during my first few years at the market, and still more who have inspired me to grow as an entrepreneur and filmmaker. It's amazing what you can learn if you simply keep your ears open and listen to what people have to say. This book would not be possible without every single person who's offered help along the way, so, thank you all.

I would not be where I am today without the guidance of many teachers and mentors. All of you helped me to become the person I am today and helped make this book possible. George, my AFM Guru, spent many hours talking to me and helping me to better understand the market. His only condition for sharing this information was that I pass it on. George, a big part of the reason I wrote this book was to share the philosophies and knowledge I've learned from you and others, as well as those I have discovered through personal experience.

First among the teachers that helped to shape me is my first producing teacher, Bill Brown. Bill, you were the person who convinced me to start going to AFM, which I mark as the moment I became a real producer. Additionally, you taught me the core rules of entrepreneurialism and being a truly independent filmmaker. I can honestly say that without you I would not have the career I have today. So thank you.

Jim, we met after the first edition of this book was published. But through the time I've spent developing ProductionNext with you, in the slightly more than a year since we've been working together, ProductionNext has helped me further my goal of connecting Silicon Valley and New Hollywood. You understand my continual need to write and publish, and are understand of it helping to move all of our goals forward. So from the bottom of my heart, thanks.

Randy, Producer Foundry was new when I wrote this book. It's not, anymore. I want you to know how much your continued friendship and advice has meant to me. As well as our silly slack and Facebook chats. Thank you so much for doing all of the cover design on all two, three, or four books I've written, depending on how you draw the line at editions.

Tony Wilkins, you were the person who originally convinced me to write this book. You served as a valuable cheerleader, coach, and mentor along the way. Your friendship and guidance mean the world to me, and some of the advice you have imparted has ended up within these pages, particularly in the "Developing a Personal Brand" section of the book.

To Rebecca, you keep me sane. You edited this second edition in a single afternoon, after I rewrote all 55,000 words in 6 days. So thank you for that. A bigger thank you for always being there when I need to talk, and helping me to step away from the computer and stop working.

To Evan, I hope you know how much your friendship means to me. It's more than just the professional relationship that it was when this book was first published. You shot the 7 Secrets video series with me, and now you co-host the Film Insight Podcast. Further, you were an initial participant in the DudeBro Movie night. Watching movies with you and Alex are great ways to spend an evening.

Speaking of Alex, I'm not sure where to start. As the other in the DudeBro triad, as well as a karaoke family member and the editor of the podcast and both of my audiobooks, thank you from the bottom of my heart. My life is much better with you in it. Also, thanks for re-editing the book top to bottom while I was trying to convince my publisher that first editions have a lot of the same content as second editions.

Alaina, your content editing have been invaluable in helping to further refine this book back in the days of the first edition. You always answered your phone through some of the publishing challenges and shared resources that helped to get this book out on the market.

Darva, you're a valuable client, advisor, and friend. Thank you so much for transcribing the interview with Daisy and correcting my terrible syntax and grammar. Seriously, I know you spent hours on it. It made a huge difference. I don't think you realize how much your support from the very beginning as the first speaker I ever booked for the IIFF truly means to me. So thank you.

Marc, thank you for the foreword. Your support and cheerleading through my various business endeavors is truly appreciated. Also, your continued efforts to mentor not only me, but all of San Francisco's up-and-coming producers you come in contact with is truly inspiring. You are a tremendous asset to our community, so thank you for everything you do. You embody the change we want to make with Producer Foundry. So thank you.

Debbie, I'm not sure where to begin. I suppose I should start by thanking you for the Preface. But there's more than that. Thanks for believing in me from when we first met. And thanks for being our first workshop presenter. It means a lot to have the faith of an industry veteran such as yourself.

Tom Marcoux, thank you for guiding me through some of the marketing challenges and your valuable suggestions to beef up the marketing for the challenge that is independent publishing. Having the counsel of someone with your experience is truly appreciated.

Chris Solemna, thank you for Photoshopping the cover image. It was an idea on a whim and you made it look truly awesome.

Kevin Hayden, thank you for taking the photo that became the cover and always being a supportive friend. Further, thanks for always being able to lend an ear. I hope you and your family are happy in Sacramento.

Gunz, thank you for tolerating my incessant complaining while writing the book, occasional bouts of writers block and overwork, and helping me to further refine the cover. Your support means the world to me. You are a true friend. Despite the fact we don't talk much any more, I want you to know that I still value the time we had together.

A very special thanks to all the distributors, sales agents and financiers who contributed to this book, especially Daisy Hamilton. The interviews, emails, and support you've shown are greatly appreciated.

To Gary Tomchuk, while we never talked much about AFM, your outlook and approach to business has greatly influenced mine. You helped to define and better some of the philosophical underpinnings of my approach to all things related to business. Your coaching and support mean the world to me.

Thanks to all my staff who have attended AFM with me to learn the ways of the market, and were part of the inspiration for writing this book. This goes double for Cha. Even though we no longer work together, it makes me happy that you still come to the market and get business done. Also thank you Cha for loaning me the pitches to share within these pages.

Lucas (Daniel) Dougherty, thank you for the invaluable fashion advice you contributed to chapter 9. I truly appreciate your input in a topic that I don't know as much about as I probably should.

Sheridan, Thank you for giving me the first review, which Is now on the website. You were the first professional contact who read the book, and getting that review was a huge confidence boost in finishing the book.

Joe, you are a trusted advisor and confidant. Your support and advice means the world to me. Thank you.

Dexter Mahaffey, I have no idea whether you'll ever read this book, but you were the first teacher to ever support my writing and helped to put me on the path that eventually lead to me going to film school. I always struggled with writing due to my dyslexia, so the support you gave me in

High School gave me the confidence to continue writing and eventually write this book. So, from the bottom of my heart, thank you.

Dori Weiss, I hope you read this book one day. You were my first real film teacher and contributed greatly to my path towards writing this book. So thanks.

Steve Moos. I shot my first films under your tutelage. So if I'm tracing this back, then you deserve a mention. Please continue the great work you do introducing High School students to media production. There are few better at it.

I must also thank every single speaker I've worked with in the various incarnations of the seminars and panels I've put on. I've had the privilege of learning from you all and tidbits here and there have been included in this book.

I'd also like to thank all the members of Producer Foundry. We've built a strong and vibrant community that supports and educates filmmakers. The support you've all shown from such an early stage helped remind me that this book was worth writing and worth finishing.

Last but not least I need to thank my parents. Your support is much more than most parents would have given. I'm not sure I could ever fully thank you for all the support and guidance you've given me throughout life. I love you, and I hope this book shows that your support lead to something.

ABOUT THE AUTHOR

Ben Yennie is the Founder and CEO of Guerrilla Rep Media, and founder at Producer Foundry, a business school for Independent Film. He is also the Co-Founder and VP of Business Development for ProductionNext, a cloud-based, film-specific project management suite that makes managing projects easier. Find links for that in the resource package.

Formerly, he was Chapter Leader for the Institute for International Film Finance for San Francisco, Vancouver, New York, and Los Angeles. While there he hosted and organized many seminars on film finance, and screened business plans for an elite group of angel investors known as The Film Angels.

He has attached well-known talent to projects, including Jodelle Ferland of Twilight: Eclipse and Claudia Christian of Babylon 5. He co-ran a Kickstarter campaign that raised more than 33 Thousand dollars, and has secured multiple six figure distribution deals while in the script stage. He has also sold projects to several PayTV outlets, and sub-licensed many projects to distributors and sales agents.

Additionally, he is the Co-Host of the podcast Film Insight, and a contributor to IndieWire, HopeForFilm.com and Cinesource Magazine. He's appeared on the #1 Filmmaking and Indiefilm Podcast on iTunes, Indie Film Hustle as well as Film Trooper Podcast, and been featured in the Deseret News and CNN Money. He's also served on various committees including efforts to brand San Francisco Film, and helped to organize a rally to bring better film tax incentives to California. He studied at The Colorado Film School and The Academy of Art University. He makes his home in San Francisco and aspires to help bridge the gap between Silicon Valley and Hollywood.

A NOTE ON SOURCES

Most of the information contained within this book is personal experience, gained from stories told by many people throughout my time at AFM. Those stories where no source is mentioned refer to information gleaned from one of many people talked to on the floor of AFM, from a presentation in a public forum, or taken from personal experience.

The information in Chapter 12 about the number of films produced every year is from a report put out by the Sundance Institute.

The contract negotiation in Chapter 16 is taken from a Ben Yennie & Associates LLC contract, and does not reveal any confidential information.

The advice from distributors and sales agents is used with permission, and taken directly from an email chain. The Interview with Daisy Hamilton has been edited for grammar based on the original recording.

While I have spoken to Managing Director of AFM Jonathan Wolf about this book, it is not officially or unofficially endorsed by AFM.

CPSIA information can be obtained
at www.ICGtesting.com
Printed in the USA
LVOW10s1019140917
548729LV00014B/189/P